Jo-Anne Vandermeulen pr ers.
*I've learned a lot by si *
her ene
—DONALD JEF
Sci-F

I highly recommend this lady ... She delivers and in spades.
—ELIZABETH BENNETT, Author and Consultant, Peer Abuse Know More!

... takes the mystery and guesswork out of book promoting, freeing up a writer time to write! —STUART ROSS MCCALLUM, Author of "Beyond my Control - One Man's Struggle with Epilepsy, Seizure Surgery and Beyond"

An absolute waterfall of information! Well done. —J. W. NICKLAUS, Author of The Light, the Dark, and Ember Between

... a great job helping writers learn how to promote their work. That is so essential today. —MARYANNE RAPHAEL, Author of "What Mother Teresa Taught Me" and 11 other published books

Everything you say is true. I am glad that I used your services, as I was banging my head against a solid wall of confusion before. What you accomplished for me would have taken me years to learn, if ever.
—JAY MILLER, Author of Inspirational Children's Literature

... you have so much good info here. I'll be coming back to read more.
—G W GRESHAM, Author of Thriller Fiction

... helps me understand that there is more to this than just putting thoughts down on paper. —APRIL FICEK, Local Saskatchewan Aspiring Author

Great organization. You're so dedicated to your craft, and dedicated to writers. Props, gal. Smiles.
—KELLY MORTIMER, Owner and Agent, Mortimer Literary Agency

Great info Jo-Anne ... I've tried to explain this same concept so many times. It's not hard to apply, and I know you have helped a lot of people with your excellent information. Thank you for that.
—ADRIENNE SMITH, Good News Merchant

JO-ANNE VANDERMEULEN

Practical Marketing Ideas To Create Massive Exposure And Drive Traffic To The Site Where Your Books Are Sold

PREMIUM PROMOTIONAL TIPS
FOR WRITERS

www.premiumpromotions.biz

The Laurus Company
Denton, Texas USA

I give credit and thanks to all of the bloggers and marketing experts who have generously taken time to share their wealth of knowledge with others like me.

PREMIUM PROMOTIONAL TIPS FOR WRITERS

PUBLISHED BY THE LAURUS COMPANY
POST OFFICE BOX 2071
LAKE DALLAS, TX 75065 USA
www.TheLaurusCompany.com

EDITORS: Nancy E. Williams and Diana L. Meadows
COVER AND LAYOUT DESIGN: Nancy E. Williams

Copyright © 2009 by Jo-Anne Vandermeulen

All rights reserved. No part of this book may be reproduced in any form or by any means, electronic or mechanical, including photocopying, recording, or by any information storage and retrieval system, without permission in writing from the publisher, except for brief quotations in critical reviews and articles.

ISBN-13: 978-0-9841680-4-0
ISBN-10: 0-09841680-4-4

PRINTED IN THE UNITED STATES OF AMERICA

Premium PROMOTIONAL TIPS for Writers

A "must-have" resource book filled with practical online marketing tips for those who have products to sell.

Although this book was written for writers promoting their books, these promotional tips can be applied to any products you may wish to promote via the Internet.

You will learn how to target your audience, create massive exposure, and drive traffic back to the site where your books or other products are sold.

Acknowledgements

This book would not have been possible without God's grace. He has given me a second chance. Never take things for granted. What is here today can be gone tomorrow.

> *"Losing an ability doesn't have to be a devastation. I have learned to conquer all obstacles, to count the blessings, and to hang on tight as the momentum increases and takes me on a journey I could never have imagined."* —Jo-Anne Vandermeulen

A special thanks goes to:

My editor, publisher, and dear friend, **Nancy Williams**, and co-editor, **Diana Meadows**, of *The Laurus Company*. Nancy designed the cover and the page format to turn a non-fiction resource into an easy sight on the eyes (pun intended).

My business partner, **Brian Knight**, is another necessary appendage to my life—always around to steer *Premium Promotional Services* in the right direction with clients when I'm unavailable. His easy-going demeanor is so necessary when I'm frazzled. He is a man with a genuinely HUGE heart.

My assistant, **Pamela Thibodeaux,** is a mini-me at Premium Promotional Services. She offers knowledge, compassion, and the same quality of service for our clients. She filled my shoes many times during my last book tour and the creation of this book.

YOU! This book, *Premium Promotional Tips for Writers*, is possible because of you. Your words of encouragement, support, and shared knowledge, fuel my body, giving me the energy necessary to gain speed. God bless you all.

table of contents

Acknowledgements 7
Table of Contents 9

INTRODUCING ...

Jo-Anne Vandermeulen 13

GETTING STARTED

You Have Written A Book ... Now What? 17
Deciding How To Publish. 17
    Traditional Large Publishers 17
        Traditional Large Publishers *You Do The Math* 18
    Small Publishers 19
    Self Publishing 20
What Can I Expect An Editor To Do?. 22

MOTIVATION FOR MARKETING

Promoting Your Name and Your Book 23
Jo-Anne's Favorite Sticky Note Motivators 26

TIP #1 CREATING MASSIVE EXPOSURE

Turning Nightmares into Pleasant Dreams. 27
Social Bookmarks: Get Noticed Now! 29
Read It, Read It, Read All About It! 32

TIP #2 BUILDING AN AUTHOR PLATFORM

So You Want To Sell Your Book. 34
Who Likes To Get Naked?. 35

Building A Strong Author Platform 37
Jo-Anne Vandermeulen's 13 Tips On Building
   An Author Platform 39

TIP #3 TARGETING AN AUDIENCE

Creating a BUZZzzz 46
Where Do I Find My Audience?
   Jo-Anne's Favorite Social Networks 47
Bring Your Viewers To You
   Jo-Anne's Favorite Free Classifieds 48
Targeting for Mountains Instead of Molehills 49

TIP #4 BLOGGING

To Blog or Not to Blog ... That is The Question 51
Blog the Right Way 52
10 Successful Points to Creating a Blog
   Your Readers Will Love 53
Successful Blogging in 7 Simple Steps 54
Field Guide To Blogging 56
Professional Blogging 61
Jo-Anne's Tips for Presenting a Professional Blog 63
Finding Your Niche 64
Content Is The Key 65
A Delicious Post Devoured in One Bite 67
Long Tailed Keywords 68
Links: Functioning Blogs/Websites 71
Fueling the Search Engines 74
Are You Breaking the Law Without Knowing It? 76
Jo-Anne's Favorite Blogs or Blogrolls 76

TIP #5 DRIVING TRAFFIC

Convert Streams to Flowing Traffic. 77
Jo-Anne's 10 Sure Ways To Draw Viewers to Your Blog. . 78
An Attractive Blog/Website Generates Traffic 79
Jo-Anne's 7 Tips on How To Post. 80
Podcasting: Promoting through BlogTalkRadio 81
Climbing To The Top: Search Engines 83
Turn First Impressions Into Loyal Followers 85

TIP #6 SOCIAL NETWORKING

Marketing and Promotions: Top 3 86
Twusted Twitter Twools and Twips. 88
How To Sell Books 91

MARKETING AND PROMOTING

No More Fear 91
The 5-W Marketing Plan 95
Learn From the Best 98
Scams: Beware of the Swarming Sharks. 101
Leave the Promoting to Someone Else 104
Exposure, Exposure, Exposure! 107
Book Distributors. 108

INTERVIEWS WITH JO-ANNE

An Interview with Sharon Ball 112
An Interview with NouveauWriter. 116
Where You Can Find Me 122

GLOSSARY

Glossary 124

introducing...

Jo-Anne Vandermeulen

JO-ANNE VANDERMEULEN graduated from the University of Saskatchewan with a degree in Education and a major in English Literature. For 20 years, she enjoyed a full life raising her two daughters as a single mom and working as a full-time teacher. That left little time for fulfilling her lifelong dream of writing.

At the age of forty-two, Jo-Anne's life drastically changed. She was diagnosed with a medical illness that sent her home from the classroom.

Determined not to let this devastation ruin her life, she used the unplanned turn of events as an opportunity to fulfill her dream. In just seventeen days, Jo-Anne wrote her first novel, a story that was unbelievably self healing.

Since that time, Jo-Anne has met and married a wonderful man who supports her writing passion, and her second book, a romantic thriller titled *Conquer All Obstacles,* has been published. She has welcomed her new career, the journey to publication, while developing an expertise in the promotional industry. Now having the time to pursue her writing and develop her goals, she has:

- produced four completed novels in addition to this non-fiction resource you are presently reading, *Premium Promotional Tips for Writers,* which was pre-requested by thousands of followers. The first book Jo-Anne wrote is still awaiting publication, but her second fiction novel, *Conquer All Obstacles,* was published and released in September 2009. It is getting rave reviews;
- created an author platform—belonging to over 30 social media networks where her audience networks through her two blogs, "Free Marketing Tips for Writers" and "Journey to Publication";
- gained a wealth of experience through attending writing conferences, participating in online workshops, gaining membership in several writing associations, and meeting publishers to pitch her first book.

Jo-Anne soon discovered that the writing and publishing journey does not stop there. After diving into online support groups and following professional bloggers, she learned the skills and techniques to successfully promote and market books. Her desire to help other authors led her to share the new information she had found in the form of posts in her "Free Marketing Tips" blog. Not long after, her fellow writers recognized her expertise and began to contact her asking to utilize her promotional services.

Yes, Jo-Anne discovered her new niche in life.

The demand for Jo-Anne's marketing and promotional services rapidly grew. Thousands of authors requested her services. A new opportunity knocked, and the door opened. All she had to do was walk through.

PREMIUM PROMOTIONAL SERVICES: *You Write – We Promote* was born—a new venture that is successfully filling the demanding gap for many authors. Her business offers the services necessary to target audiences, create massive exposure, and drive traffic back to the clients' sites where their books are sold. Endorsements can be found at:
www.premiumpromotions.biz

New media opportunities led Jo-Anne to produce and host a weekly live Internet radio show called "Authors Articulating." This BlogTalkRadio show hosts both renowned guests and aspiring authors in an energetic podcast where they and Jo-Anne discuss various promotional and writing topics, and listeners are encouraged to interact, deliver their author platform, and pitch their book.

> *"Gratification is knowing the wealth of knowledge has been shared with fellow writers."* —Jo-Anne

Along with her business partner, Brian Knight, Jo-Anne states, "Together, we have our hearts set on helping writers. We care!" She often says that "supporting authors comes naturally." Her name and brand, "Conquer All Obstacles," can be seen buzzing through many social media sites as she answers questions and responds to calls for assistance.

"You can turn devastations or unplanned events into opportunities," she beams to anyone who will listen. She has proven that *conquering all obstacles* is possible as she continues to encourage fellow writers and readers that they, too, can overcome life's unexpected tragedies.

From her home in Saskatchewan, Jo-Anne is happily living her dream come true with her husband, Randy. She is currently promoting her new books and those of her clients while she continues to fulfill her lifelong dream of writing.

Getting started

You Have Written A Book ... Now What?

*I*t has taken you months or perhaps years to write and polish your book. Don't stop now. You deserve to earn the most profit from all of your hard work, but it doesn't just happen. There are decisions to be made. Now, your book needs to be published and promoted.

Deciding How to Publish

Traditional Large Publishers

Traditionally, when we think about publishing a book, the big New York publishing houses come to mind first. We picture them handing us a nice, fat advance check as we hand over our manuscript. A few months later and, *voilà*, our book is on display in the local bookstore ... NOT!

Okay, a few do make it after a long process of submitting query letters, full and partial manuscripts, emotional ups and downs, etc., and we are very happy for them. But unless you have previously published and/or created a popular name for yourself, you are facing a long ordeal to get the big boys to even notice you, possibly years. Some people hire agents to do the legwork for them, but it carries no guarantees and is usually expensive.

The following are some interesting statistics about large publishers:

- **The six major U.S. publishing houses:** Random House, Inc., Penguin Putnam, Inc., Harper Collins, Holtzbrinck Publishing Holdings, Time Warner, Simon & Schuster, Inc.
- **Book sales in the USA:** A fiction book is considered successful if it sells 5,000 copies. A non-fiction book is considered successful if it sells 7,500 copies.

—*Authors Guild* (www.authorsguild.org)

TRADITIONAL LARGE PUBLISHER
You Do The Math!

As an author, going through the big New York publishing firms may not be the answer anymore, according to Literary Agent Nathan Bransford in his article, "Book Revenue Breakdown." (Archives, February 2009, blog.nathanbransford.com)

How much does an author receive from a book sale? Here is a synopsis from Nathan's article. All amounts are hypothetical. Discounts to booksellers vary.

$24.95 Hardcover	**$14.95 Trade Paperback**
Publisher – 50%	Publisher – 50%
Author royalty – 10% less Agent's 15%	Author royalty – 7.5% less Agent's 15%
$12.48 to the bookseller (50%)	$7.48 to the bookseller
$9.98 to the publisher	$5.83 to the publisher
(50% minus author/agent share)	$0.95 to the author
$2.12 to the author (10% of retail minus agent's 15%)	$0.17 to the agent
$0.38 to the agent (15% of 10%)	

According to Nathan, neither the author nor the agent receives a royalty check until all those little $0.95s per book have exceeded the amount the publisher paid the author in the advance.

- **Book sales by store type:** 24.6% large chain stores; 17.7% book clubs; 15.2% smaller chains and independent stores; 5.4% Internet, such as amazon.com.

  —www.BISG.org
- **Royalties:** The average royalty is 10.7% of net. The average advance is upwards of $1,500 and $7,500.

  —John Huenefeld,
  Publishing for Profit by Tom Woll

Small Publishers

Don't be afraid to consider a small publisher. There are numerous small publishers available. Getting referrals from other authors is the best idea. I highly recommend seeking references from several previous clients before making a final choice. Because a publisher does a lot of advertising does not mean they are reputable or can produce quality books.

Most small publishers will be able to handle the technical aspects of preparing your manuscript for printing. Many have editors and designers on staff, work with Print On Demand (POD) printers, and offer distribution through major distributors, such as Ingram. And small publishers are often more accessible to the author.

Although you will have to pay as you go for editorial, design, and printing services, there are some small publishers who are quite reasonable, depending on how much work is involved in polishing your manuscript.

There are benefits to working with a small publisher.

- **More control:** The author retains ownership and has a say in manuscript edits and the design process. He can manage sales avenues, coordinate bookstore consignments, and distribute his book through as many sources as he wants.

- **More royalty to the author:** Small publishers usually pay higher royalty percentages to the author. Since you are working as your own agent, there are no agent fees.
- **Earlier release date:** Books usually go into the publication process right away, rather than waiting a year or more.
- **Flexible printing options:** Small publishers are able to work with the printing resource that is right for you, whether it is traditional printing for large quantities or Print On Demand (POD) for smaller minimum orders (as few as one), easier reprints, and quicker turn around times.
- **Longer life:** Your books will remain on the (virtual) shelves indefinitely.
- **Simplified submissions:** Small publishers will usually request full manuscripts, skipping all the steps of partial submissions.
- **International distribution:** Some small publishing companies are set up to distribute your book(s) and e-books internationally.

Self Publishing

Self publishing usually describes the process of an author producing, marketing, and promoting his own book. If an author decides to self publish, he must purchase an ISBN, hire an editor, a book designer and typesetter, have books printed, and develop a marketing plan for selling his books.

Authors who self publish retain complete ownership and control over their book. A word of warning ... Many of the larger bookstores and bookstore chains will not carry books from self-published authors. If being in the bookstores is one of your goals, it's better to go with a large or small publisher.

> *Record numbers of self-published books have been reported in 2009.*

Why is self-publishing gaining in popularity over the traditional method of publishing?

- Traditional publishers are reducing their client intake, making it even more difficult to break into a highly competitive market.
- Due to rising unemployment, people have more time at home to pursue their dreams of writing.
- High-speed printing and binding machines have made publishing relatively inexpensive compared to the high cost of traditional offset printing. (Offset is still viable for large orders.)
- Self publishing gives you flexible options based on your own needs and desires. You can decide on each step of the process, whether to handle it yourself or contract it out.
- Abundant "how to" resources are readily available to guide self-publishing authors in effectively handling all stages of self publishing, including promoting and advertising.
- Most of your customers are online, so you can market from home targeting a larger audience base. We will show you how in this book.

So which kind of publisher is right for you? Only you can make that decision, but be prepared to invest the time and work required by the option you choose. You should also be prepared to make any needed course corrections. If your first plan leads you down a dead-end path, be prepared to look at other options. This happened to me.

My path toward a large publisher became completely blocked. For me to see my novels in print, large publishers were not the answer. I had to turn around, scan for more publishing options, and venture down another path. I was able to *conquer all obstacles* by going with a small publisher and learning to handle my own marketing and promoting. Looking back, I know it was the right path for me.

> *You can self-publish, reap the profits, and spend your time doing what you love—writing.*

One of the major reasons writers went to traditional methods of publishing in the past was for the marketing and distribution resources provided by the major publishing houses. This book, *Premium Promotional Tips for Writers*, will give you the tools you need to be able to promote yourself and your book(s) across the World Wide Web. It is not difficult! If I was able to learn how to successfully market myself and my books, so can you!

You, too, can *conquer all obstacles*.

WHAT CAN I EXPECT AN EDITOR TO DO?

Basic Copy Editing – Any or all of the following:
- correcting spelling, grammar, punctuation, syntax (grammatical arrangement), and word usage while preserving the meaning and voice of the original text
- checking for or imposing a consistent style and format
- reading for overall clarity and sense on behalf of the prospective audience
- querying the appropriate party about apparent errors or inconsistencies
- noting permissions needed to publish copyrighted material

Substantive or Line Editing – Includes all aspects of Basic Copy Editing (above) in addition to improving a manuscript in any or all of the following ways:
- identifying and solving problems of overall clarity or accuracy
- reorganizing paragraphs, sections, or chapters to improve the order in which the text is presented
- writing or rewriting segments of text to improve readability and flow of information
- revising any or all aspects of the text to improve its presentation

Thanks to my editor, Nancy Williams of The Laurus Company, for providing this information. For more information about editors, go to: www.thelauruscompany.com/editors.html

Motivation for marketing

Promoting Your Name and Your Book

Before starting the venture into marketing research, I avoided anything to do with promoting like the plaque. Although I had the interest and viewed other writers' websites, authors' blogs, groups' home pages, and my daily incoming emails, it was only with flitting glances of curiosity. I would quickly scan over an article and move on to another facet of writing. You may wonder why.

Before I answer, I must ask you: Are you ready to face your fears?

Fear is the first major obstacle to conquer.

It was a mysterious thing to me, this daunting marketing and promoting business. My fear caused me to avoid educating myself. I was afraid of the unknown, I feared failure, and I was terrified of throwing myself off balance—*too much to do and too little time to do it.*

Still, like a haunted house, it stood there beckoning me. The main door opened, taunting me to enter. I remember my curiosity as I faltered into this strange place, my constant chants of internal coaching:

"A change of attitude ... I can do it ... one step at a time ... easy does it, Jo-Anne."

Does this sound crazy, or can you relate?

Advancing into the first room, I began to discover the reason for marketing and promoting. For the first time, I came to an astonishing realization:

> ***You don't need to be published in order to market.***

You are losing valuable time if you are waiting until your book is published to begin talking about it. Most of what I read encouraged the writer to make himself known and to advertise his book in advance of publishing ***(Tip #1—Create Massive Exposure)***. The best way to do that is by introducing yourself to others and giving them a taste of your writing long before your release date ***(Tip #2—Build An Author Platform)***.

Reading further, I learned that I needed to gather a following of potential buyers ***(Tip #3—Target An Audience)***, so that when my book hit the stands, I would have an audience waiting. I was amazed to read that Internet users number over two billion. What an incredible number of people! I concluded there was no better way to promote myself and my book than through the Internet.

The reason for promoting had been planted, and the possibilities were endless.

> ***Reality hit me in the face. There is an unbelievable potential for growth ... all within my control.***

I trudged through the second door of my fearful haunted house and discovered that blogging was not as difficult as I had imagined ***(Tip #4—Blogging)***. I created my first site, roamed the Internet, and joined groups. The next lesson I learned was how to point my growing network to the site where my books are sold ***(Tip #5—Driving Traffic)***.

I quickly gained a following, and surprisingly, these followers became my friends—a community of fellow writers sharing and supporting each other *(Tip #6—Social Networking)*.

What first started as a self-serving reason for promoting soon became a rewarding experience each and every day. Even to this day, I meet so many wonderful people who give me the greatest gifts—their time and their presence.

I had kept a rough journal of my adventure, and looking back, I noticed that in a short amount of time, I had *conquered all obstacles*. My fears were gone, and I had found confidence in being able to sustain balance in my life.

> *My fears were gone, and I had found confidence ...*

I have gained so much through this journey of learning the strategies of marketing. I have found understanding, insight, and the support of so many people. I'm grateful to have found the courage to face this house of uncertainty and to have wandered through the front door.

Looking ahead into the future, many other doors will open, and I will probably wander through them. I surely cannot pass up the new and wondrous opportunities because, really, there is nothing to fear but fear itself.

It thrills me to share with you the promotional tips I have learned. May these tips encourage you that you, too, can *conquer all obstacles*.

Jo-Anne's Favorite Sticky Note Motivators

Do you keep quotes stickied to your bathroom mirror? In front of your toilet? In your car? Some of you are chuckling and nodding your heads. I find it is good to plan ahead for those times when we are feeling down and need a little motivation. The positive messages scrawled on my sticky notes give me what I can't find within. There are millions of inspirational slogans we can use to pull us up from a dark hole. Here are some of my favorites:

"When one door closes, another one opens."

"Go with the flow."

"Keep your eyes open for the unexpected. Don't be afraid. Seize the opportunities before you."

"You have your own answers within you."

"*Everybody is talented, original, and has something important to say.*"
—Brenda Ueland

"**Imagination is the Divine Body in every Man.**" —William Blake

"*Be careless, reckless! Be a lion, be a pirate when you write. Why you are not to be discouraged, annihilated, by rejection slips.*" —William Blake

....

Sometimes, it is great just to know we are not alone. We all have a bad day every now and then. Have you ever caught yourself staring at an empty screen with a completely blank mind? The creativity isn't there. Here are a few suggestions from famous people:

"Moving around is good for creativity: the next line of dialogue that you desperately need may well be waiting in the back of the refrigerator or half a mile along your favorite walk."
—Will Shetterly

"Stopping a piece of work just because it's hard, either emotionally or imaginatively, is a bad idea. Sometimes you have to go on when you don't feel like it, and sometimes you're doing good work when it feels like all you're managing is to shovel shit from a sitting position."
—Stephen King

"Writing books is the closest men ever come to childbearing."
—Norman Mailer

Tip #1 Creating massive exposure

Turning Nightmares into Pleasant Dreams

*I*magine yourself on a dark stage in the largest theater hall in the world. Everything is quiet. The curtain lifts. Suddenly, the light is blinding. Before your eyes, you have over a billion people cheering in the crowd. They are waving money in the air, chanting for you to speak about the work of art that is tucked under your arm—your book.

What if I told you this is not a dream?

You are on stage. There are over a billion customers out there waiting and wanting to find you.

Second quarter of 2008, the Census Bureau of the Department of Commerce stated that the total number of Internet users worldwide was 1,463,500,000 viewers, 7 days a week, 24 hours a day.

Even though we are living in tough economic times, people are still spending money. Your customers are waving money, wanting to purchase your book.

But right now, there's a problem ... your customers can't find you. They don't even know you exist. Suddenly, this wonderful dream has turned into a nightmare. The curtain lifts and you are looking out into a theater hall that is empty. All is quiet, and you are alone.

When your curtain lifts, what do you see? Are you living a dream come true, or are you tossing and turning as the nightmare continues?

> *Within the second quarter of 2008, retail sales increased by 0.9% over the first quarter of 2008. This is equivalent to $1,034.8 billion USD.*

You do not have to be one of the many talented writers who goes unnoticed. Your book does not have to be one of the many books that gathers dust on a shelf, never to be sold.

Question: So how do you navigate over a billion Internet viewers to witness your outstanding performance?

Answer: Through promotional tactics, proper website fundamentals, and learning strategies and techniques on how to market and sell your book through the Internet.

There are keys to success when it comes to marketing your book online:

- Create a presence.
- Target your audience.
- Create a buzz.
- Drive traffic.
- Provide evidence that your book is a must read.

If you have the time, energy, and knowledge, you can *conquer all obstacles* and make the profits you deserve when selling your book. Rest assured, you can have pleasant dreams and wake up with a smile on your face.

> **The higher your ranking in the search engines, the greater the chances that your potential customers will find you and your book(s), and the greater chances you will have of successfully selling your books.**

Social Bookmarks: Get Noticed Now!

I am going to share a HUGE tip that will allow you to hit over a hundred social bookmarks with just one click (okay, make that three clicks). First, there are some very important techniques that must be in place to ensure optimized search engine success.

Have you updated your profile lately?

Search engines are drawn to keywords or tags like a magnet. The webcrawlers will snag your name and the specific topic you are promoting as long as you have completed the following:

1. **Completely fill in your profile on search engine sites.**

Make sure you have completely filled in your profile on search engine sites, such as Google, Yahoo, and MSN. Check your profile by going to these sites:

Google: www.google.com/profiles

Yahoo: profiles.yahoo.com

MSN: home.live.com - Click on Profile.

Help others search for you easily. Your followers can enter your name into these three popular search engines and discover where you are: your site location and the updated content you have posted on your blog. Optimize the search engines. You must do the footwork. After this, you can sit back and let the "feelers" do their job.

2. **Update your profile in your social media networks.**

Update your profile in your social media networks, e.g., Facebook, Myspace, Linkedin, Goodreads, ShoutLife, etc).
This may seem like a lot of work, but it is well worth it.

Usually, the first place your curious viewers will investigate to learn more about you is in your profile. Take the time to post a picture, share your interests, and make sure you include links back to your main blog or website. This is the perfect place to display your book cover and a short synopsis. Be inviting and encourage your viewers' feedback.

3. Announce your new content.

When you have written a new post to your blog, the social media networks such as Twitter and Facebook are the perfect places to submit a short announcement about your new post. Include the specific link so your viewers can have direct access to your blog/website.

This will be attractive on their homepage as they will be able to view your picture and the illustration you've chosen to publish with your article.

On other social media networks, such as NING, make sure you click the RSS feed on the side widget and type in your site address. Automatically, your completed published posts will appear right on your profile page.

4. Social Bookmark your newly published posts.

Social Bookmark your new published posts. First, ping/bookmark/tab/ your original published page on your blog/website. Second, go back into your social media networks and Social Bookmark the page again. The webcrawlers will go crazy with excitement and feature you even higher in the search engines. Here are the 2 social bookmarks I use that save me tons of time and energy:

1. **www.pingmyblog.com** – Copy and paste your new page into the "Blog URL box," give your page a title, click on the bottom box that says, "Check All," and, boom, you have now hit over 70 social bookmark sites with just one click.

2. **feedshark.brainbliss.com** – Again, go through the

same procedure as above: Click the "Enable Submit Button," then click "Submit Now – Chomp, Chomp, Chomp," and *voilà*, you have now hit another 36 social bookmarks in one shot with only a couple of clicks.

The more consistently you post, the more excited the webcrawlers become. Realistically, I cannot afford to dedicate all of my time to blogging, so I post two new articles with solid content per week.

Where do I spend most of my time? Do I social bookmark every article on every page?

Yes, this is where I do spend my time, and it is worth it. Setting the webcrawlers in motion creates immediate results. My name and topic soar to the top of most search engines. Try typing "Jo-Anne Vandermeulen" or "Conquer All Obstacles" into one of the search engines—Google/Yahoo/MSN—and see where I show up. Am I on the first page? You bet! Heck, I might even be #1!

So what is my secret?

There is no secret really. Just follow these procedures:

1. Create a deadly post with awesome content.

2. Send out bursts of short announcements to friends and followers who are now fans on Facebook and Twitter.

3. Encourage any visitors who come to the site to sign up for a FREE subscription. Automatically, new articles will show up in their email.

My followers love it!

And you know what this means? They will share their knowledge with others, just as I have done. They will tell two friends, who will tell two friends, and so on, and so on.

Good luck and remember …

YOU can *conquer all obstacles*!

Read It, Read It, Read All About It!

Now you get to be a fly on the wall.

Whose wall?

The wall of everyone who is talking about you.

How?

Sign up for the two Alerts below and fill in the keywords. So simple and cool. Automatically, these Alerts will provide you with the names of those who are talking about you or your books.

> **Google Alerts**: www.google.com/alerts
> **Twitter Alerts**: www.tweetbeep.com/

Why is this important?

- This information will tell you if your webcrawlers are working and if you have chosen wise tags (keywords). If the alerts are sending you your own pages that you have social bookmarked (added to Delicious, Digg, Bookmarks, StumbleUpon, etc.), it means you are doing a great job with your internal links.

    I have been a guest blogger on some other sites, and the alerts sent me that person's site with my name quoted. I can then send this information back to the presenter and let them know their internal links are active. Chances are, they are ranking high in the search engines.

- Alerts has sent me quotes of mine that I've caught others using. Whether you call it stealing or copyright infringement, it is wrong. Others should never take words from someone and claim them as their own without giving proper attribution. GRRrrrrr!

- I use Alerts to reveal how effectively my promotional/marketing techniques are working. Whether I'm promoting myself or a client, my plan is to create massive exposure. I expect Alerts to pick up "Jo-Anne Vandermeulen," "Conquer All Obstacles," and "Premium Promotional Services" every day. If I don't see the Alerts picking up my tags, then I know I'm not doing my job. I need to reactivate my internal links and social bookmark my pages. This is why linking blogs with other active bloggers is a great idea. When they social bookmark their page, your tags will automatically be marked and sent to Alerts. That is a double win.

"Great site, Jo-Anne. Great progress and, for lack of a better word, "great" reading. I like everything you said and some of the things you didn't say. I have been writing most of my life and getting published for over 30 years and love it. Some of the things you posted are exactly what I say to newcomers. I noticed a link to my web page on your homepage. Wow, thanks; no wonder my book sales have gone through the roof."

—Dr. Robert E. McGinnis

Tip #2 Building an author platform

So You Want To Sell Your Book

An author platform will quadruple your readership and sell your book. What is an author platform? Think of a *platform* as something to build upon. Picture a platform standing several feet off the ground. We are now going to build a visible presence on it. What is that visible presence we are going to build? **Everything about you and your book.**

> *An author platform is where you tell the world about yourself and your book.*

Before I share some valuable tips with you about building an author platform, I would like to address a few questions.

What if my book is not yet published?
Don't wait. Now is the time to build your community. The larger the audience, the more your publisher/agent will like it.

What if I don't have a blog or website or even know what a large community network is?
A platform can be built one step at a time. Heck, I didn't know anything before I started, and now I'm writing a book.

It takes time and commitment, but what worthwhile endeavor doesn't? Once you begin and find an interest (who is more interested in you than you?), it seems more like a hobby than work.

When searching for a book to purchase, do readers look for the title, the content, or the author?

Before your book hits the stands, you must network and generate followers who will search for you, the author. Then they are interested in what you have to say.

Why do some authors sell so many books while others barely receive any blog hits, comments from viewers, or interest in their book?

Even though authors venture out to book signings and pursue personal promotional opportunities by networking, they may not have applied the strategies that turn their blog into a network haven. You are about to discover how a few simple strategies will help you create a profitable website or blog. I will show you the one simple way to increase sales. You don't have to be a professional web/blog designer to sell your book!

Who Likes To Get Naked?

GOTCHA!

A great title can capture an audience's attention …

And now that I have your attention, I'm going to focus on AUTHOR PLATFORMS—the reason why every writer should spend time designing a bragging article about who he or she is and what it is they write about.

In a bookstore or on the selling page of a site, your book sits among thousands of other books. Your blog/website hovers in cyberspace, naked, among millions of others.

"We keep hearing this phrase, 'What's the platform?' Well, what it is is this: What does the author bring to the table? Talent is not enough. The number of slots open to fiction on a publisher's list is being reduced all the time."
—Literary agent **Nat Sobel**, quoted in *Poets and Writers Magazine*.

Unless effectively promoted, it will sit shivering and all alone. You and your book will blend in with the other authors and cover jackets like a chameleon taking on the appearance of its background.

Solution: You need to put on some clothes. And I mean dress really well. You need to stop hiding from all the viewers and come forth. Building an impressive author platform is the solution.

> *Particularly for a debuting novelist, the publisher needs something to make that book stand out from the thousands of others, something that will make the novel get noticed, and purchased—a platform.*

An author platform is more than a bio. Just as a real platform elevates a speaker above his audience, you must discover ways to make yourself and your book stand out from the crowd. Present yourself as Cinderella in the eyes of the Prince. Your platform must stand out from all the others.

This is not the time to be humble. You must really look at yourself in comparison to the other authors in your genre and discover what makes you and your novel unique. Cinderella presented herself in a beautiful gown. Her beauty stood out from the crowd of possible prospects for the Prince. For you as an author, what descriptors hook the viewers' attention? Use both your character and your process of writing. Expose who you are and your voice. Really look at your work. What are your strengths? What captures your audience and keeps them wanting more? Be creative in your response. Show your voice in the explanation.

To *conquer all obstacles*, you have to sell yourself.

It is time to strip off your artistic wardrobe and squeeze into a business suit. It may not feel comfortable, but it is necessary to attract viewers. This is not the time to blend into the crowd. Writing is art, but publishing is business, and business is about making money. Whether it is the author, publisher, agent, or you as a self-publisher, your book must sell in order to make money.

An author platform sells!

Building A Strong Author Platform

Know Your Target Audience

It is always the **writer's responsibility** to get to know their audience by filling in the blanks and accumulating a specific description. Areas to look at include:

- Genre
- Age
- Ethnic background
- Classification (student, working, retired, etc.)
- Interests, Hobbies, and Lifestyles
- Perspectives, Attitudes, and Values

Meet The Needs Of Your Viewers

Times are changing. Flexibility is the answer in today's business world. What worked yesterday may not work today. Think of targeting the market. Needs and interests are turning around. Promotion is never stagnant, and neither should your message be. Set aside some time to:
1. Constantly revisit the brands and messages used to **hook your audience**.
2. **Analyze the successes and strengths**. Build on the strengths rather than focusing on the weaknesses.
3. **Make the necessary changes** to enhance your marketing tactics that work well with potential customers.

This will generate more traffic to your site and convince potential customers to buy your books.

Take a good look at your message. Does it give the viewers what they are searching for? Are you in sync with your audience? This may take further research. It takes time, but it is more than necessary. If you want to *conquer all obstacles*, you are the one who must be flexible and tap into their needs.

> *The message you post must persuade viewers that you and your book are unique and stand higher than the rest.*

Staying Out of the Slush Pile

You must present a strong author platform to get the attention of an agent, editor, or publisher. They want to read in your query letter who you are, where you are established in the writing world, and how you are planning to market and promote yourself and your books.

I want to share with you my recent experience:

I decided to submit one of my blog posts to **Ezine Articles**. I wasn't looking for cash payment but for publication credits to elevate my author platform.

To my surprise, my article, "Turning Nightmares Into Pleasant Dreams," was immediately accepted and published. I also earned **Expert Author** status. Now doesn't that title sound pretty impressive in a query letter?

As an added bonus, I was given notice that my article would appear on their high-traffic home page. Bonus! So, now I have exposure.

Building an author platform is similar to keeping past positive references from previous employers. You can *conquer all obstacles* by submitting an article or post from your blog to a publication or e-zine. It is a simple and painless way to build credits and show the experts just exactly who you are … a fabulous writer.

Jo-Anne Vandermeulen's
13 Tips On Building An Author Platform

1. Use Blogger if you are inexperienced.

If you are an inexperienced blogger, then Blogger(.com) is very user-friendly. It is also free.

My second recommendation is Wordpress. Their support team is wonderful! Wordpress.org comes with a yearly fee but gives the owner more control over the HTML code. The owner can load the code onto their hard drive and then manipulate the code to change appearances. There is more flexibility and control using Wordpress, but it is not necessary. KISS—"Keep it simple, sweetie." It gives the owner a free site and enough control to get by. One of my own websites is on the wordpress.com platform: www.joconquerobstacles.com.

Caution: Many widgets cannot be included in the wordpress.com platform. When I first blogged with Wordpress, there were problems with the appearance from one browser to the next. The posts looked fine when viewed in Mozilla's Firefox, but when viewed in Internet Explorer, there were fragments of HTML code within the normal text. To fix the problem, Wordpress support instructed me to copy my posts from the Internet Explorer browser and delete the HTML code that was showing. After doing this step for quite a few months, I checked Internet Explorer one day and there was no HTML code showing. I suspect that Wordpress fixed this problem.

2. Infuse links to increase traffic.

Tap into many blogs and websites that interlink to bring attention to the author.

Example: I requested permission with Pat Bertram to link our blogs together. We now share followers.

Caution: View the site carefully before agreeing to link.

3. Always leave your signature, brand name, and address.

Always leave your signature with your promotional brand name and your website/blog address.

Example: Jo-Anne Vandermeulen
Conquer All Obstacles
Prolific Writer of Romantic Fiction
http://www.joconquerall.com

Limit your signature to four lines or less. You never know who will copy and paste your link or make a comment on your site or theirs.

Caution: If you don't have anything nice to say in a comment, don't say anything at all.

4. Invite, invite in your social networking sites.

Twitter, Facebook, Ning, MySpace, LibraryThings, Shelfari, Goodreads, ShoutLife—remember to target your reading audience and request other people to be your friend. This enables them to read your posts and vice versa. Create bio or profile pages that are attractive and positive. Try to leave the reader with something they can have or contribute towards.

Example: I leave my followers with advice and encouraging words of wisdom.

Caution: Groups can get ticked off if you promote yourself rather than staying on topic or discussion. Read the group's objectives or seek permission before advertising your blog or website.

5. Make it easy for followers to subscribe to your blog.

Near the top sidebar, have an easy to submit spot for your followers to subscribe to your blog. Placing the word FREE promotes others to follow. Do not forget to have a link to your

RSS Badge. You can Google "RSS Badge" to learn more.

Example: I have my picture (or, if you're published, your book cover) on the sidebar. Directly under it, I have my FREE button for subscriptions and a link button.

Caution: Do not clutter your sidebar. Stick with a maximum of five categories. Delete widgets that are not used. Organize the widgets by dragging them around from your dashboard. Print you blog entries on white background with black print.

6. Include a "Contact Page."

Interaction is so important. A relationship needs to develop. Trust can come from this active communication.

Example: "Jo-Anne loves to hear from her friends, so drop her a note! Thanks."

Caution: In "Settings" make sure you can preview the comments people make prior to publishing them.

7. When you post, be sure to use your tags and link keys.

Example: I highlight a keyword, such as "Marketing," after I click on the link key and then add my URL, which is joconquerobstacles.com. I then list "Marketing" in my tag space. See my blogs and you'll see the keywords in the color purple. You will also be able to read my tag words. Click on them and see what happens.

Caution: Do not repeat tags or link keywords. You might think more would be better, but it is not.

8. Join several groups related to your line of writing.

Join several groups in your networking sites that are related to your line of writing. Market to anyone who is going to buy your product. Contribute, meet new friends, and help each other out.

Example: I am an active member of RWA, Edgy Christian Fiction Lovers, Critique Partners, Romance Writer's United.

Caution: Whatever you write is published material for the world to view. Edit your work carefully before you push the send button.

9. Clarify your niche, what sets you apart from other authors.

Clarify your niche or target group, what sets you apart from other authors.

Respond immediately to any comments. Keep the structure of your blog consistent, so followers grow familiar with its navigation. Always make it easy to read. Remember, you want others to follow you, so keep this in mind at all times when you are blogging. Back up your facts with quotes (remember to get permission and give recognition when quoting others or using their material).

Example: My titles are eye-catching: "Blog Or Not To Blog ... that is the question." I write about what interests me and what I've learned in my own journey. Then I pass this information on to others. I print short sentences with lots of spaces. Columns are easier to read. The KISS system is usually the answer: Keep It Simple, Sweetie (Silly, Stupid).

Caution: Stick with the Times New Roman font; it is easy to read. Use underlining and bold for emphasis.

10. Learn from the best.

Take a close look at blogs that have a lot of hits or have earned famous recognition through nominations. Borrow ideas and add to your own. Think of who you would like to follow and why. Use these strong traits as your guide.

Example: Recently, my blog was nominated for the Real Blog for Real People Award. In the first two months, my blog had one thousand hits.

Caution: Being specific in your topics is the best, but it will narrow down your followers. Listen to others and read the comments; follow their lead as to what they find interesting in your blog. Go in that direction.

11. Allow "Alerts" in your Settings.

Allow Delicious, Goodreads, Stumbleupon, and Blog Alerts in your Settings. Followers of these Alerts will then receive notice of your announcements, and other readers you have not even targeted will begin to visit your blog. Check out social bookmarketing sites such as del.icio.us, dig.com, or stumbleupon.com.

Example: Since I allowed Alerts in my settings, I have discovered my name/brand signature all over the place. I know others are reading it also. Even lurkers who don't reveal themselves are reading my blog.

Caution: Do not be afraid to be assertive with "fans" who are not genuine. Block them or mark as spam ASAP.

12. Link your freelance writing to promote your book.

Use your blog/website to promote your freelance writing and link it all to your book. Relate the articles to your book.

Put your site address on your business cards, create announcements using your full profile signature, send an e-mail blast to family and friends announcing your new site, and ask them to send it to their friends.

Example: Jo-Anne is a freelance author and a prolific romance writer. Announcement: "Check out my new blog post." The easiest sale is to someone you know. They will recognize your value.

Caution: Unless you have a published book, you cannot link back to amazon.com. But if you do have a published book, go for it. Keep your notes short and sweet.

13. Be creative and offer your readers something they can win.

Be creative and offer your readers something they can win—give-aways, free e-books, bookmarks. Posting your site address gives you more exposure and builds your platform.

Example: I'm giving free advice to others who comment on my blog. This will drive up traffic stats and promote my platform. That's a win-win for both follower and author.

Caution: Be honest. Do not break your promises. A good name is simple to build, but a good name lost is very difficult to regain.

OTHER FREE TIPS

- Submit your blog to blogged.com and trade blog reviews with your blogroll.
- Submit your site/blog to related directories.
- Use your RSS feed to put your blog content on Facebook, MySpace, etc.
- Use a service like Feedburner to syndicate your RSS feed and reach a broader audience. Feedburner also allows users to subscribe to your feed via e-mail. Note that Google bought FeedBurner and is converting all users. If you have not done so lately, log into Feedburner.com.
- Use apps on Facebook and other social networks to integrate with Twitter. This allows you to update your Facebook status via Twitter.
- Use Google Analytics (free) to monitor your traffic, where it is coming from (referring sites, search engines, etc.). You know how many Facebook friends you have, but do you know about how many people actually come to your website every month? How long do they stay? What content are they clicking on? You get all this and more with Google Analytics. Imagine being able to say: "I get 1,000 absolute unique visitors on my website every month, and they stay an average of five minutes. They view an average

of 4.5 pages per visit, and I have a 40% bounce rate …"
- Use Google Webmaster Tools (free) to make sure Google has no problems crawling your site. It also allows you to monitor who is linking to your pages, what keywords have been used to find you, and more.
- Integrate your blog with Twitter using the Twitter updater plug-in.
- Enjoy promoting by combining what interests you.
- Reward yourself for even the tiny steps forward.
- Watch in amazement as your audience builds and your communities expand.

> *"We look for authors who are not only great writers but are willing to promote their work and also understand the enormous changes in the industry. It used to be 75% about how good the book was and 25% about the marketing, but now it is 75% about the marketing and 25% about how good the book is."*
> —Peter Miller, Literary Manager, *PMA Literary*

Tip #3 Targeting an audience

Creating a BUZZzzz

We are not here to expand our discussion on "Who Likes To Get Naked?" It's far too cold in Canada to expose any skin. Yet, even in Saskatchewan, it is acceptable and more than necessary to show off our ... bo ... boo ... BOOKS!

No one is going to know about your talents if you publish and then hide the covers among all the others in a bookstore or cyberspace. Marketing your books and promoting yourself is a must.

> *I want to promote myself, show the world my writing and/or published books, but where do I start?*

- **Target your audience.**

    You must define your target audience. For this book, my target audience is writers and authors. If you have a non-fiction about dogs, for example, you will search for groups of people who discuss dogs. If you're a fiction writer, you may want to hang out around fiction readers. Narrow it down some more, and become a member in groups discussing your specific genre—mystery, historical, etc. Ask yourself: *I want to sell my book, so where do I find my consumers?*

- **Create a buzz.**

    You can *conquer all obstacles* through networking, but first you need to discover where your viewers are located on the Internet. Unfortunately, when you first begin to promote your author platform, the viewers will seldom come to you. It is your job to go to them, introduce yourself, allow them to taste your writing. Once you have established friendly contact, then you have to keep them coming back over and over again. First impressions are important, but a good first impression does not necessarily mean you have hooked them to purchase your book. A sense of trust must be established. A personal connection.

WHERE DO I FIND MY AUDIENCE?

Listed below are social networks that target writers and authors. These resources or groups are shown as widgets on the sidebar of her blog front page.

Jo-Anne's Favorite Social Networks

- **Red Room**
- **Gather.com—Groups**: Gather Books Essential/Publishing Outside of Gather.
- **LinkedIn**
- **FaceBook—Groups**: The Smoking Poet, Suspense/Thriller Writers, Writers Helping Writers, Authors Promoting Authors, Facebook's Poets and Writer's Registry, Readerjack.com, Writers Resources on ijustfinished.com, GLBT Writers and Readers, Writing Papers Single Spaced Makes My Double Spaced Result Climactic.
- **GoodReads—Groups**: Tips on Self Promotion, Sales/Advertising/Published Authors/Book Trailers, and Author Websites/PPS Book Title Promotions.
- **AuthorsDen**
- **Book Marketing Network—Groups**: Novel Authors and Publishers, Christian Authors Connection, Author Support, Self-Publishing, Free Book Marketing, Non-fiction Authors and Publishers, Marketing in the United States, Book Publicity.
- **LibraryThing—Groups**: Writer-Reader, Bloggers.
- **Shelfari—Groups**: Authors Promos.

BRING YOUR VIEWERS TO YOU

Wouldn't it be easier to have the viewers come to you? You bet! I would not rely completely on posting advertisements, but there are viewers out there who search the ads for their interests. It's your job to make sure you are listed.

Jo-Anne's Favorite Free Classifieds

- **USFreeAds.com**—Account signup required. You can post up to 10 free ads. Upgrades available, $9.95 per month upgrade for unlimited ads. You can use HTML and pictures with upgrade. Ads post for 40 days with a renewal option. Offers an Affiliate Program.
- **ClassifiedAds.com**—Account signup required. Unlimited free ad posting by country. No HTML or pictures. Ads post for 30 days with a renewal option.
- **InetGiant Account**—Signup required. Unlimited free ad posting. No HTML or pictures. You can choose add-ons for minimal charges. Also offers Web Blaster and Ad Blaster for an additional charge. Offers an Affiliate Program. Ads post for 30 days with a renewal option.
- **Sales Spider**—Account signup required. Unlimited free ad posting to a state and city. No HTML, pictures allowed. You can "feature" your ad for an additional charge. Also offers a Business Center, e-mail, forums. Ads post for 30 days with a renewal option.
- **Free Ad Space**—Smaller advertising site. Account signup required. Unlimited free ad posting. Add-ons available at a minimal cost. No HTML, pictures allowed. Ads post for 6 months with a renewal option.
- **Hoobly**—Account signup required. Unlimited free ad posting. No HTML, pictures allowed. You can choose Premium for minimal charges. Ads can post up to 6 months with a renewal option.
- **Adland Pro**—Account signup required. Unlimited free ad posting up to 255 characters. No HTML or pictures. Different upgrades available. Also offers a Business Center, e-mail, forums. Geared toward affiliate marketers, with resources and tools available.
- **US Net Ads**—No account required. Unlimited free ad posting. No HTML, pictures allowed. Ads post for 4 months with a renewal option.
- **Classifieds For Free**—Account signup required. Unlimited free ad posting up to 100 words. No HTML, pictures allowed. Ads post for 14 days and are renewable.
- **Craigs List**—Account signup required. Ads posted to city only. Unlimited free ads. No HTML or pictures. Craigs List will not allow any links or websites to be posted or any duplicate ads.
- **Web Cosmo**—Account signup required. Unlimited free ad posting. HTML allowed, pictures allowed. Ads post for 90 days and are renewable.
- **Pressmania**—Account signup required. Unlimited free ad posting. No HTML, pictures allowed. Ads post for 90 days and are renewable.
- **Ad Post**—Account signup required. Unlimited free ad posting up to 200 words. No HTML, pictures allowed. Ads post for 30 days and are renewable.
- **Free Classifieds**—Account signup required. Unlimited free ad posting. HTML allowed, pictures allowed. Ads post for 6 months and are renewable.
- **WebLeg Free Classifieds**—Account signup required. Unlimited free ad posting. No HTML, pictures allowed. Ads post for 60 days and is renewable.
- **Subblurbs**—Account signup required. Unlimited free ad posting. No HTML, pictures allowed. Ads post for 60 days and is renewable.
- **Flugpo**—Account signup required. Unlimited free ad posting. No HTML, pictures allowed.
- **Readerjack.com**

Targeting for Mountains Instead of Molehills

*I*magine seeing vertical peaks in your blog or website stats that bring a smile to your face. Not often in life do we anxiously anticipate mountainous vertical slopes. Wouldn't we rather face the molehills? Not when we open our dashboard and click on "stats."

Whether we are talking about our main site where the potential customer can purchase our books or the blog we use to generate our following, the main goals are to increase our following and to keep those viewers coming back.

*How do we **conquer all obstacles** and get that line on the visual graph within our stat page to keep climbing?*

Create Great Content
- Structure, facts, grammar, spelling, and punctuation do play an important role, but there is more. **The content must have feeling and an underlying logic that flows and is easy to absorb.**
- The content must be filled with emotions that challenge the reader and can lead to a powerful call to action. **Provoke an emotional response from the reader.**
- Discover that balance between communicating the truth, challenging the reader to understand your message, and producing facts without coming across as dry. **We want to produce content that is interesting, challenging, and informative.** Give the reader something they can take away with an "aw" or "wow" experience. Don't hide important information, thoughts, or steps, but don't toss it in their lap either. Reread your post before publishing and omit unnecessary words. Try it and be amazed at the results.
- The most important thing in content marketing is to be **reliable.** You must produce the goods or content consis-

tently, or the readers will not show up. The molehill will have prevailed. The plan is simple. **Schedule your posts, be genuine to your followers, and get the content out the day you promised.**

Simple Strategies That Will Generate New Readers and Keep Your Original Readers Coming Back

- **Remind the reader to subscribe.** Remember, there are newbies coming to your site all the time. Sure, you posted the directions initially, but it doesn't hurt to post the simple instructions again. I do this at the bottom of the odd post:

    "Interested in having Jo-Anne Vandermeulen 'Conquer All Obstacles' bi-weekly posts automatically deposited in your Inbox? Please subscribe for FREE by clicking on the button on the side of this blog."

- **Send or post an invitation to subscribe and to invite a friend. Viral promotion generates readers.**

    "Send this to a friend: Please, e-mail this to a friend. [Place your photo of an envelope.] *Got a friend that could use some tips on marketing and promotion for themselves and their books? Forward this email to help them Conquer All Obstacles."*

    "If you received this email from a friend, subscribe to 'Conquer All Obstacles' HERE [link your site]."

All of this sounds incredibly easy, but it works. My stats have looked more like mountains than molehills.

Creating a buzz means mingling with your targeted audience. Reaching out to your viewers is the most effective technique to promote. Posting your work allows your viewers to find you. You must make a presence to *conquer all obstacles* and promote successfully. So simple.

Tip #4 Blogging

To Blog or Not to Blog... That is the Question

Creating a blog in Wordpress is FREE and simple. Developing character for your blog is like "sharpening your sword."

Plow into the design, hover over the lingo, and don't be afraid to push buttons. Learn as you go. You can always change it later.

Why would I need a blog if I'm not published?

After attending the Muse Conference and reading the forums, I discovered the purpose for having a blog. You create a blog to sell yourself. A writer must generate a following so that when that novel is published, your fans will be more responsive, interested, and more apt to purchase the book.

If you wait until you are published, it may be too late. The best time to start a blog is NOW.

Just think about the billions of people who will get to know who you are from Internet communication. It kind of puts the hours of sitting in bookstores signing covers into perspective, no?

What qualifications are necessary to create a blog?

If you know how to type, you can create a blog. But if you want to increase interest (hits or visitors) in your site, that takes a little more knowledge in the advertising department and the technical areas.

A lot of blogging tips can be found on the Internet. Google the keywords "blogging tips" in quotations. It will show you in simple, easy to follow directions everything you need to know about blogging. Here is a specific site: www.squidoo.com/expertblogging

How do I attract more interest and hits to my blog?

Like any advertisement, your blog should be attractive. It should have purpose and be informative. You should make it easy for visitors to subscribe. **Branding**, or developing a theme, along with a logo symbol will trigger your followers' memory. The more they see your brand/logo, the greater the chances they will remember you. You have to build trust if you want your followers to gain enough interest in you to buy what you write.

I encourage you to create a blog. Delve into the unknown, and sharpen your blade as you go.

You can *conquer all obstacles*.

Blog the Right Way!

*I*s there a correct way to blog? That is much like asking if there is a right way to write.

Actually, outside of using correct grammar and punctuation and conforming to fact or truth, any form or action of writing that expresses and communicates the writer's intent to their audience is acceptable.

"Correct" is a subjective term in the realm of advertising and promotion. There are, however, better ways if one is to follow the advice of experts who have tested their theories and proven them successful.

If your objective in blogging is to generate traffic that will put you and your book in the spotlight, then take heed to the following points:

TEN SUCCESSFUL POINTS TO CREATING A BLOG YOUR READERS WILL LOVE

1. **Write in conversation style.** Make it easy to understand and enjoyable to read.
2. **Choose a clean design, with no distractions.** There are many templates. Choose one with a clean design.
3. **Use short paragraphs.** Include bullet points, headings, and subheadings. It will be easy to scan for information.
4. **Keep blog posts short.** If needed, set up a link to long reference material.
5. **Have a plan and stick to it.** Plan your topics, how to market, and scheduling in advance. It shows commitment.

Fact: *Blogs can take up to 6 months to gain a steady group of readers unless you market your blog consistently. Promote to advertise and attract readers.*

6. **Create links to past relevant and popular posts, and ones that introduce YOU.** Easy navigation will make your new readers more comfortable with your site.
7. **Produce valuable and unique content.** Learn/entertain/update. Your readers must get something out of reading your blog.
8. **Establish a sense of community.** Interaction will make your readers feel a part of your blog.
9. **Brand yourself.** Discover your niche and use this tag in your signature and the theme of each post. It will create a tremendous gain in popularity through search engines and will attract new followers.
10. **Always include an "About" section and a "Contact" page** with your contributing post page.

Conquering all obstacles does not mean to get caught up in a web of perfection. What one reader may see as valuable, another may view as a waste of time. The most important aspect of blogging is for you to write. Relax. The more comfortable you are in expressing your voice, the more often your audience will revisit your blog.

Successful Blogging in 7 Simple Steps

You have decided to blog. Wonderful! Blogging is a learned skill. After a few posts, sit back and ask yourself these questions and carefully consider the answers.

- **Why am I blogging?** To create an author platform.
- **What am I hoping to gain from blogging?** Followers, i.e., fans, potential buyers who will revisit my site.
- **Who am I targeting for a viewing audience?** People who are interested in my genre.

7 simple steps to help perfect your blogging skills:

1. **How's that title working for you?** A headline has less than a second of a site visitor's attention, so it must be compelling. The title must catch the viewer's attention and draw them into the rest of your post. Is your title short and worded to benefit the reader?
2. **Include a picture.** Images will hold the viewer a tad longer than a page filled with straight text information.
3. **Break up the information.** Include subtitles and/or highlighted key words. The viewer can scan and stop to read if something interests them. Again, KISS—simple is better.

4. **Let your voice ring true.** Be real. Conversational or informal language is more friendly and will hook your audience. Share experiences and interesting information to show credible authority. Can you open yourself to show vulnerability? Transparency works wonders—draws attention, gains trust, and gathers true friends. Don't forget to display a photo of yourself. Our brains are wired to create relationships with faces.

5. **Choose a topic.** To decide on the area or content for your article, research past stats to check where your audience lingers the most, what topics have the greatest hits, and which posts gathered the highest number of comments. But don't let that stop you from taking a chance. Slip in just one post that waivers from the usual and see what happens. Adding flavor doesn't hurt. And you never know, another door may open.

6. **Put your best stuff up top.** Did you know the top of the page gets about 17 times more exposure than the areas near the bottom of the page?* If 40% to 50% of the viewers leave your blog after the first page, take your best first step forward. Don't leave the best for last. Think of this as a sprint instead of a long distance race. Present your best information first and in a tight manner.

7. **Presentation is everything.** My husband hates when I say this, but it's true. First impressions are lasting impressions. I have discovered by reading through several subjective comments from site reviewers that most readers do not like music, flashy pictures, and wallpapered backgrounds. **A site that is simple to navigate and read will attract viewers.** Again, KISS is the key ingredient to an attractive site—KEEP IT SIMPLE, SWEETIE.

Ask yourself again … ***What is the purpose of my blog?*** If you have designed your blog to build an audience, you must serve the viewers. Now the blogging isn't about you, it's about them. When it's time to make your next post, read your content through their eyes.

Reference: Step 6 facts collected from ClickTale Blog article, *ClickTale Scrolling Research Report V2.0 - Part 2: Visitor Attention and Web Page Exposure.* http://blog.clicktale.com/2007/12/04/clicktale-scrolling-research-report-v20-part-2-visitor-attention-and-web-page-exposure/

Field Guide To Blogging

What are the advantages of blogs?

- **Multi-Functional.** A blog can work as a website. A tab at the top of the blog site can guide the viewer to your web page.
- **User Friendly.** You feel more in the driver's seat. A blog is easy to create, and you can do it yourself with no HTML skills. You don't need special software or an expensive web designer.
- **Timely.** By updating regularly, you can stay current with the needs of your audience.
- **Interactive and Personal.** A blog is a great way to stay in touch with your readers in a more informal manner. The audience is involved by submitting comments. You can generate a following with this connection. Discover what they want and delve into the requested direction of their interests or concerns. YOU get more exposure through marketing yourself and your book(s).
- **A Showcase of Your Ability.** You write, and they read for themselves your awesome abilities, style, and voice.
- **Free.** Many blog hosts are free.

- **Higher Search Engine Exposure.** A blog provides more exposure for you. Using links and tags, each keyword will pop up in search engines.
- **Easy to Maintain.** Through expert technicians, free and quick assistance is there if needed. They will provide answers to any questions and solve any concerns.

What are some of the popular blog platforms?

Think of a *platform* as something to build upon. That's why we have *author* platforms and *blog* platforms. We are building. If you are not computer savvy, the terms can become confusing.

A blog platform actually refers to the program you are using to build your blog. I would need to be experienced in using many different blog platforms to recommend the best. I am using Wordpress for "Conquer All Obstacles," but we have chosen Blogger for our business site, Premium Promotional Services.

Popular blog platforms are:
- Wordpress
- Blogger
- Typepad
- Tripod
- Squarespace

What kinds of things should I have on my blog?

You must ask yourself:

What type of blog do I want to write?

If you want to promote yourself and your book, your blog should contain the following:

1. First/Feature/Home Page

First impressions are lasting impressions. Highlight your Home page with posts and information your followers will find useful. Empathize with your target audience. The key to promoting yourself or your book is understanding your customers and their buying habits.

Your focus will determine the content of your first/feature/home page. You may even decide to have your bio or a synopsis of your book as your first page. You have control of the steering wheel. If at all possible, however, I recommend not advertising your book on your feature page. People need to feel they can trust you before you pitch your book.

Invite a message by making it easy to leave a comment.

2. Sidebar and Widgets

- If you want to promote yourself and/or your book(s), make sure you show your picture and/or the cover of your book on the sidebar of each page,
- Place the following widgets on your side bar(s).
  - A friendly and professional photograph of you. Link the photo back to your bio page.
  - A badge your followers can click to subscribe. Easy to follow instructions: "Click here for your FREE bi-weekly subscription."
  - Your book cover. Link this to another page where you detail information, i.e., About/Price, etc.
    (*Note: Wordpress does not allow you to advertise, so you may want to use Blogger as your platform if you are selling your book.)
  - A search space. I use Google plus my own search button for easier navigation.
  - List of Blog rolls.
  - List of Groups you belong to.
  - Categories. List no more than 3 to 5.

- List of Recent Posts.
- List of Resources.
- List of Writers, usually fellow writers sharing links.
- Archives.
- Recent Comments.
- Meta or Log In button.
- Subscribe RSS button. Very important so you can link your other blogs together.
- Blog stats. (This is questionable. It could be a negative if you are not getting many hits.)

View the dynamics of your blog to make everything look user friendly and attractive. Do not clutter the page.

Make your blog look professional by using a black font on a white background.

Keep it simple. No fancy flashing buttons, music, or slow-to-download animations.

Remember, your audience is there to read your material; they may not have a lot of time. Give the reader what they are looking for right away. The fewer clicks needed to find your material, the more welcoming your site becomes.

Maintain cohesiveness throughout your site. Use the same format and structure throughout.

View other sites and ask yourself what you like or dislike on their pages. There is nothing wrong with borrowing ideas.

3. Other Pages

- **Author Bio Page:**
  - The four main questions your viewers want answered from your bio:
    1. Who are you?
    2. What is your expertise?
    3. Can your expertise address my problem or goal?
    4. How can I contact you?
  - The most viewed page on any website is the About Us page. People want to know who you are. Sell yourself.

- ✓ Present an eagerness to talk about yourself and your work.
- ✓ Write in third person when appropriate.
- ✓ List facts, not wishes.
- ✓ Cite relevant information.
- ✓ Write tight. Limit to three to four sentences.
- ✓ Add a hook.
- ✓ DO keep your professional bio as short as possible.
- ✓ DO be selective; it is not necessary to list your entire professional background.
- ✓ DON'T include information that is not relevant to your audience.
- ✓ DON'T be bland. Let your personality show.
- **Contact page.** Make sure people know how to reach you.
- **Promotional page.** Don't forget the purpose of your blog.

How can I help people find my blog?

- **Search Engines** – The key is to get your name listed at the top of the search engines. You need a brand, keywords that are repeated often in your content, links, and tags.
- **Marketing** – Constantly post your "signature" everywhere: in forums, blog comments, and emails.
- **Self-Promotion** – Promote your site. Advertise in MySpace, GoodReads, FaceBook, Ning, BookMarketing, MyLogBlog, Twitter. Promoting is time consuming and must be done constantly to be effective.
- **Paid Promotional Services** – If you are tight with deadlines or want to focus solely on your writing, you may want to consider hiring someone to build your author platform and promote your book. There are a few promotional services available if you search for them. One of them is my own company, **Premium Promotional Services**. For more information, see page 126 or visit us at: www.premiumpromotions.biz.

Professional Blogging

> *How do I create a blog that "conquers all obstacles" and stays out of the slush pile?*

"The Internet is a vast wasteland of thoughts and ideas. According to Technorati, someone creates a new blog every 1.4 seconds. If blogging was a crime, and in some cases it very much should be, it would be the number one source of criminal activity in the land."
—Adam Brown, FreelanceSwitch.com Site, 1/07/09

> *Top Priorities for a successful blog*

With these alarming facts, how do I create a blog that someone will choose to read?

1. **Be prepared to market and promote your blog.** Invest the time needed.
2. **Present your blog in a professional and user-friendly manner.** It must have eye appeal to your viewer.
3. **Target your audience**. Submit relevant, factual, and interesting information that invites reader comments.
4. **Discover the balance between selling and presenting.** Feel comfortable expressing yourself. Have fun writing. It will show in your voice.
5. **Edit.** Polish each post. Make sure you have included all widgets necessary for your viewer to navigate comfortably to gain the knowledge they seek.

There are a few things you may not be aware of that, left unchecked, may leave a bad taste in the mouth of your audience. And unfortunately, it may take only one of these to turn a viewer away forever.

> *"Remember, as the medium becomes more and more mainstream, there will be more and more blogs and more and more opportunities."* —ProBlogger, Darren Rowse, 03/21/09

In the corporate world, the presentation of your professional blog may soon be seen as a reference tool that reflects who you are. The content and presentation of your posts honestly exposes your expertise and can open doors for many new opportunities, even in areas you may never have dreamed.

You can *conquer all obstacles* and open the doors of opportunity by blogging professionally.

> *"If you can establish yourself as the blogging expert in your niche, not just a blog writing expert in your niche, there is money to be made from a fertile market."*
> —ProBlogger, Darren Rowse, 03/21/09

Jo-Anne's Tips for Presenting a Professional Blog

To help guide you in creating a fabulous site, check off the following items as you carefully evaluate your own site.

_____ **Type properly using capitals and lower case.** Do not use abbreviations or shortcuts. Use proper capitalization in your title. Do not leave entire sections in bold print. Do not leave words like "i" in lower case.

_____ **Use the word "blog" correctly.** Do not call your post or article a "blog."

_____ **Spell names correctly.**

_____ **Avoid rambling.** Keep your content short, specific, and relevant.

_____ **Keep your readers informed.**

_____ **Use pictures to spice up your post.**

_____ **Establish yourself as a source of information.**

_____ **Keep your posts positive.** Bad mouthing and constant complaining is just plain unacceptable.

_____ **Related Posts.** Choose a maximum of 2 or 3 previous posts to place at the end of your article. Do not include a string or list of related posts. KISS.

_____ **Take blogging seriously.** Invest the time and attention needed to be successful.

Finding Your Niche

Are you worried about positioning yourself high in the ranks on media sites? Perhaps you shouldn't.

Social networking is all about establishing a territory for yourself, not necessarily defining it. Focus more on your business and less time obsessing about your positional ranking on media sites. This will keep your eyes open for new opportunities. If you are focusing only on your ranks, you may be missing out on some valuable opportunities.

If you establish a territory, it will be difficult for others to dislodge you from that position. So keep your attention on your business and selling your books.

Defining a defensible position in a profitable niche can be compared to playing a game. The team that scores the most points at the end is the one that wins.

Take a dose of *courage* and intensify your niche. Presenting yourself as authentic will generate an even larger loyal audience. Be *creative*. Nothing is better than when your viewers can identify with you and feel your personality.

Ask yourself, "What makes me stand out from the rest?"

Devising a strategy to remain on the offense takes critical thinking, but if you can relate this to a game, it is simple to understand the reason. You can only score if you play offensively.

If you want to *conquer all obstacles*, you must show everyone who you *really* are. Be open and true to your viewers.

Position your territory and intensify your niche.

Content Is The Key

Quality matters! Enhancing your followers' lives will gain you respect and credibility and will produce even more followers.

You have a keychain full of keys. They are heavy, pulling down your arm, jingling as you step. A closed and locked door is in front of you. This door is your blog, and there is only one key that will unlock the barricade that is obstructing your view.

Which key will open the door?

1. **An impressive title?**
2. **Optimized search engine links?**
3. **Consistent posts?**
4. **Great content?**

If you chose **number four**, **great content**, you have discovered the key that will open the door.

Now you step into the room, and what do you see? A crowded room full of followers. But they are a tad restless. Thousands of heads are turning and eyes dart around looking for the nearest exit. Many glance at their watches. They obviously don't have time to stick around. Oh, no, they are heading for the doorway. Quick, act fast!

How do you keep your audience from fleeing?

No! Don't shut the door and lock them in. No one likes to be trapped. Don't throw your content at them or keep what you know a secret. Instead, use your elegant voice to communicate wholeness around the message that matters the most to you. Smile and relax into the content that brought your followers into the room in the first place. **This is the time to prove your credibility.** You have to earn their respect.

Invite your guests to sit down. Offer them refreshment. Show your interest in them. Ask questions. **Interaction is a must.** Heck, they may agree to link your blog with theirs.

Your followers have come to your blog for a reason.

You have provided great content in the past. They are hungry, needing to feast on information they can use. Serve your guests the fine food you have been busy preparing. Present the delicacies on a fine silver platter. Give them a choice of which aromas they wish to taste.

By providing quality content, your guests will probably talk about their experience after they leave, sharing their memories with their friends of the fine morsels they received in your room ... oh, I mean your blog.

Word of mouth—viral promotion—goes a long way!

The most important key to opening the door to success is to produce a blog with great content. Give, give, give your followers what they've come searching for. Don't hold anything back. Yet, be careful. The content must be current and researched properly. The information must be accurate for the post to have quality.

Quality matters. Enhancing your followers' lives will gain you respect and credibility, which will produce even more followers. How does this happen? It happens through viral marketing, the use of communications networks that are already in place. It is the best marketing method ever—friends telling friends, word of mouth—and it's free. When a follower reads something they like, they will tell their friends and associates, who will tell their friends and associates ...

A Delicious Post Devoured in One Bite

Providing great content that is infused with perspective and background to make it pleasing to the reader.

Too many writers who blog serve a plain, fried hamburger. Sure, it will attract the hungry viewers, but once they are full, they will wander away. Unless they are starving, the chances are good they will discover a more appetizing meal down the road and never return.

Most people can eat fried hamburger, but it is rather bland on its own. By adding onions and a few spices, the taste is much more enjoyable. Garnish the plate with sliced tomato and parsley, and you have created a first-class meal.

Like published posts for a blog, it takes more than fantastic content to entice the reader. **A post must be relevant, fresh, and creative.** To give smart solutions to a readers' significant problems, you must provide the zing that meets their need.

Liven up those taste buds. The trick to creating a tasty post is **mixing the ingredients**—blend the meat with the spices to create a delicious meal. You know what it takes to make your mouth water.

Great food, fabulous company … now what else could a person want? Oh, yes, **conversation**. Dinner just would not be dinner around my house without the usual table talk. **Readers want content they can talk about.**

You have supplied the main course—the **meat** the reader wants. These are the **facts and smart solutions** to their significant problems. Sprinkle in the **spices**, and you will have added in **personality and style**. That is the **fun and interesting content** to stimulate the brain. Now **serve the meal with love**, rolling in the **respect and care** the reader deserves. The conclusive message will meet the reader's true appreciation and have them coming back for second helpings.

By taking the very important facts highlighted above, you can *conquer all obstacles* by creating a delicious post.

In just one bite, the reader will devour the post and be left feeling full and very satisfied.

Long Tailed Keywords

How do I optimize my search engine ranking?

You can *conquer all obstacles* by carefully selecting the keywords you are going to use in your title, throughout your content, and insert in the tag section. **Your ultimate goal is to boost your name and your site higher in the search engine ranking.**

To optimize your position in the major search engines:

1. **Register your site.**

2. **Supply great content.**

3. **Select great long tailed keywords.**

You must be asking right about now, "What in the world is a long tailed keyword?" Think about what someone would type in a search bar. A short tailed keyword might be the single word, "author," which would result in thousands of pages of search results. A long tailed keyword might be "author of romance novels." The long tail keyword defines the kind of author and narrows the selection category and the number of pages.

Selecting great long tailed keywords also works with your

blog posts and begins with your title. A catchy title will attract the readers but may remain invisible to the webcrawlers.

To make both happy, try mixing your titles. One day, think outside the box and supply catchy titles. The next day, use more descriptive or technical words.

I used the more descriptive and technical words for the title shown here. "Long Tailed Keywords" may sound interesting for those who are searching for information on keywords, but those who are reading for entertainment may just scan the title and pass it by. My blog post using this title was designed to attract the webcrawlers and boost that post high into the search engines.

Even though my site is registered and I have created great content, my objectives are clearly defined in the title itself.

A past post, and one of my favorites, was called "Turning Nightmares Into Pleasant Dreams." It was a catchy title for the reader but would probably get missed by the webcrawlers. "Links: Functioning Blogs/Websites," however, will snag the webcrawlers' attention, boosting that article higher in the search engine findings.

On the World Wide Web (www), the material is massive. Out there, we are competing with hundreds of thousands of other similar topics. The ultimate goal is to be noticed by a potential customer. When the potential customer types what they are looking for into the Google search bar (or another brand search bar), we need our name and the title of our book to be on the first page of the search results.

How do I get my name and title on the screen of a potential customer?

Our goal is to stand out from the rest and encourage the webcrawlers to scoot our name and book title as high as possible in the search engine rankings.

Carefully select the right long-tailed keywords in your

title and then repeat these long-tailed keywords several times throughout your post or site page. This will boost you higher in the search engines rankings and, as a result, drive massive traffic to your site.

Google Keyword Tool — http://www.google.com/sktool/#

Google Adwords has a very helpful tool that searches your site and suggests keywords for you to use. You can access it in your browser at the link shown above. Follow these directions or the directions on the Google screen.

1. Copy and paste your URL page link into the slot provided.
2. The Google keywords tool scans this page and suggests keywords.
3. Carefully check out the charts. A keyword such as *marketing* will receive massive clicks, but it will be impossible to compete against all the other bloggers who have also used *marketing* as their keyword.
4. If you add a string of words, a "long tailed keyword," along with *marketing*, you will see the clicks are still massive, but if you have selected strong key tailed words such as *internet marketing tool*, you are now a competitor.

Using the Google keyword tool will help you *conquer all obstacles* and win the race for standings in the search engines. Supplying the selected keywords in your title and throughout your post/page will attract the webcrawlers' attention. You will be boosting your name and title higher in the search engine rankings.

It's time to get noticed and bring attention to yourself.

Links: Functioning Blogs/Websites

I recently followed through with a friend's request to check her website and blog. Frustrated, she had asked if there was anything she could do. Apparently, she had posted great content but was puzzled when there had been no traffic. Her fabulous articles sat empty of recorded visitors. She wanted an interactive blog, a place to discuss her book with the audience. She was ready to give up, and stop writing.

Glancing through her sites, a very important component was missing. She had nothing down the sides, no added widgets and no links.

Adding links to your blog will optimize search engines and increase traffic to your site.

- **The reasons to activate webcrawlers.**

    "Turning Nightmares Into Pleasant Dreams." Like your book that sits on the shelves unnoticed, unless you draw attention to your blog, it also will just sit there unless you take action. It is imperative for the search engines to discover your blog.

- **How to activate webcrawlers so they will snag onto your blog and boost it higher in the search engine rankings.**

    "Targeting Mountains Instead of Mole Hills." Great content will draw attention, but there are other tactics that will ensure the recognition your blog deserves.

    "Keywords and Key Phrases Fuel the Search Engines." Wisely selecting the keywords and phrases and repeating them often within your site will get you more attention. But there is more …

- **External Links.**

    It is up to you to link your blog to high traffic links and maintain the links' functionality. Under the "**widget**" located on your sidebar, there is a section called "**Links**." Links are added under categories such as Blogroll, Featured Authors, Resources, etc. You can determine the title of each category and the number of high traffic blogs or sources you wish to include.
    NOTES:
    - **Proper Ethics**: Request permission from another blogger prior to linking them with yours.
    - **Add Comments**: Adding Comments to high traffic sites will establish short duration links back to your site.

    TIPS:
    - **Alexa.com**: Visit the Alexa.com site. There's a nifty toolbar you can download onto your computer. It displays a graph that monitors the actual traffic to the site you are considering for a link to your blog. There is no use linking to a low traffic site. Just watch the bar.
    - **Mashable.com:** Mashable.com is a social media guide with very high traffic. By registering and adding content (a blog post), you can link this site back to your blog. I listed it under my widget category named "Resources." I have now targeted a different audience that will branch farther out into the web and generate more buzz for my name and my new book.

    - *Never leave your sidebar widgets empty of links.*

    - Changing the term "Category" to "Title" will increase hits.
    - Periodically, **check the links to make sure they are still working.** There's no point using up space for a link that is no longer accessible. Make sure your blog remains attractive and fully functional.

- **Internal Links:**

    - *Link your own sites together.* If you have more than one blog or website, link the sites to each respective side widget. I have three blog sites:

        1. **Premium Promotional Services**
            Complete Marketing Services for Authors
        2. **Conquer All Obstacles**
            Marketing Tips for Writers
        3. **Journey to Publication**
            Jo-Anne Vandermeulen

        I make sure I have listed each site on each side bar. This links them all together. The traffic will flow from one to another, and I don't have to do anything else.

    - *Link your sites to your social media networks (My-Space, Facebook, Goodreads, etc.) and back to your blog.* Fancy buttons can replace the title and link itself, but check out the appearance of your blog after adding such buttons. Too many, too big, too flashy can distract your viewer and take away their main focus, which should be the article you've posted.

Once it was brought to her attention, my friend added her other sites and networks as links down the sides of both her website and blog. This served two purposes:

1. The audience can now follow what interests her.
2. The webcrawlers can now do their job, and traffic is flowing properly.

My friend is back writing great content articles for her blog. She is receiving the traffic she had hoped for and is now thrilled with the interaction she is having with her audience. She has even noticed an unbelievable hike in her book sales. Now she is a "happy camper" and has learned how to *conquer all obstacles.*

Fueling the Search Engines

Whether you are building an author platform or marketing your book(s), there are two main goals in creating a blog:
1. **Attract an audience.**
2. **Drive potential customers back to your site where your book is sold.**

Producing an article with great content is a must in accomplishing these goals. It is very competitive out there, much too competitive for new lurkers to just stumble upon your blog. But there are some techniques that can help to put you in the driver's seat so you can *conquer all obstacles*.

The search engine is like a limo, and you are the driver. You have prepared by filling it with the proper fuel—selective keywords and phrases. As the limo driver, you have that control. You can *conquer all obstacles*.

Never let your tank run dry.

1. **Activate the webcrawlers**: Include keywords and key phrases in your title and mix this idea with a catchy title. Think outside the box. Get those creative juices flowing. Create a snazzy title that includes keywords or key phrases.
2. **Repeat, repeat, repeat**: Sprinkle the keywords and key phrases throughout the post content without sounding robotic.
3. **Choose wisely the keywords and key phrases**: Select keywords and key phrases that your potential audience may use in their search bar (Google/Yahoo/MSN, etc.). Put yourself in their shoes. Ask yourself: "What word(s) would I type to find what I'm looking for?"
4. **Be specific** – Using the word "author" will make it very

difficult for your potential buyer to find you, but using the phrase "inspirational author" helps narrow down the search. I suggest using your name with your genre. Now we are talking.
5. **Fill in the tags**: Add these same keywords and key phrases as tags at the bottom of the post and again on the directed social bookmarks (Digg/Stumble/Delicious, etc.).

> *Write for readers first and search engines second.*

A headline has less than a second of a site visitor's attention. So, your title had better be good.

When I think of a topic for my blog post, I usually sleep on the title. Well, not literally. It's like after completing a manuscript. The idea or writing needs time to cool. In posting an attention grabbing article, the idea, especially the title, needs time to simmer. I happen to do my best thinking in REM.

When or how do you come up with your compelling blog post titles? Just one more idea if your muse is sleeping … *Blank page, I shall thwart thee!* Flip open the newspaper or a magazine article and check out the title.

A compelling title will *conquer all obstacles* by catching the attention of the reader and drawing them into the post. After all, is it not the title that gives the reader a reason to read what you have to say?

Take the time necessary to be creative. The words you choose in the title may be the "do or die" to your next blog post.

> *Some bloggers try to write titles that are so optimized for search engine optimization that they forget their actual readers. It's possible to have a post that ranks really well in Google but is so poorly worded that even though it ranks #1, nobody will click on it. Keep readers as your #1 priority.* —ProBlogger Darren Rowse 05/23/09

Are You Breaking the Law Without Knowing It?

If you are using images from Google for pasting into your blog posts, you may be infringing on copyrights.

It is very important to make sure you are not infringing on any copyrights when choosing images from the Internet to use in your blog or website. Google has a general disclaimer that says, "Image may be scaled down and subject to copyright." Webcrawlers also catalog the images on your site. So why risk a lawsuit when there are other image sources available that are free or very low cost?

One alternative source is Flickr.com. You can find simple and beautiful photos for your website that you can use legally without violation of any copyrights. But if you find an image you want to use, read the surrounding copy to make sure there are no copyrights listed. Beware of "Creative Commons" images, which have certain types of licensing restrictions. You should read through the Creative Commons link on the Flickr page to learn more.

www.flickr.com/search/advanced/

Another site that lists several free sources of images is:
www.blogsessive.com/blogging-tips/free-images-for-blogs/

Jo-Anne's Favorite Blogs or Blogrolls

- **The New Author**
- **Copyblogger**
- **Feedblitz**
- **Freelance Folder**
- **Freelance Switch**
- **Daily Blog Tips**
- **Problogger Blog Tips**
- **Nathan Bransford**

(Blogrolls are mentioned on the sidebar, as a widget to the blog.)

Tip #5 Driving traffic

Convert Streams to Flowing Traffic

How would you like to turn a few viewers into thousands of followers?

Flowing traffic to your blog or website increases the opportunities to sell your book.

To *conquer all obstacles* and gain readership for your blog, you must:

- **Be proactive.**
- **Make a constant effort.**
- **Reach your audience by getting out there.**
- **Be ready to roll up your sleeves and persevere.**
- **It will take time, so have patience.**

I guarantee that all of your hard work will pay off. The rewards are priceless. With flowing traffic heading back to your site, your book will gain attention.

With flowing traffic comes a much greater chance that you will sell your book.

Jo-Anne's 10 Sure Ways To Draw Viewers to Your Blog

1. **Produce amazing comment replies.**
   Visit other blogs in your niche or area of expertise, and leave well-written comments that contain valuable content. Leave your signature. Follow the discussion.

2. **Provide a solution; it goes a long way.**
   Get out to other social media sites and prove you are an expert. Scan the discussions for questions you can answer simply. Contribute by sharing similar experiences, and empathize with the participants.

3. **Publicize your articles.**
   Gain "Expert Author" status by submitting excellent articles from your blog. Ezine.com is one of many examples of recognized published postings (article directory) that not only attracts viewers, but is another method to get your name and niche out there.

4. **Guest post or contribute articles on other blogs.**
   Each stream comes with its own readers. Many streams turn into a flow of traffic back to your site.

5. **Build your list of followers.**
   Reach out into various social media networks and gather friends. Interact to form trusting relationships.

6. **Vary your source of posts by incorporating audio and visual podcasts.**
   Presentation is everything. Create catchy titles with eye-drawing photographs. Supply the captions and posts with links back to your site. Include long tailed tags/keywords.

7. **Target the 3 largest media sites.**
   YouTube, Facebook, and Twitter are the going fad today. Leave your signature with your site link. Update your profile within the joined media site. Interested participants will want to know more about you, so make you and your site accessible through simple navigation.

8. **Educate your followers.**
   Provide simple guidelines or reminders. Encourage your followers to subscribe and tell them exactly how. Request your followers to promote you to others (their friends). "Spread the word" or "tell a friend."

9. **Find potential new followers.**
   Know who you want to attract and where to find them. Choose sites with major traffic, and take note of where these secondary sites are linked. Vary your target audience—do not always pitch to the same viewers.

10. **Activate the webcrawlers and social bookmark each post.**
    Register your blog in Google, Yahoo, and MSN. After each post, ping the article (Digg, Delicious, Stumbleupon, etc.). Optimize your ranking in the search engines so your potential viewers can find you.

An Attractive Blog/Website Generates Traffic

You have learned to *conquer all obstacles* by reading the previous tips on how to **create an author platform** and how to **generate traffic to your site**. Now what?

> **Fact:** *"The Internet is a vast wasteland of thoughts and ideas. According to Technorati, someone creates a new blog every 1.4 seconds. If blogging was a crime, and in some cases it very much should be, it would be the number one source of criminal activity in the land."* —Adam Brown, FreeLanceSwitch Site, 01/07/09

DEVELOPING AN ATTRACTIVE SITE

Ask yourself the following important questions when presenting new posts:

1. **What will the audience get from my site?**
   Think about your target audience. Put yourself in their shoes. If you want to post in a journal fashion, you will be pouring your emotions into the post and definitely engaging yourself, but will you be involving the reader?

2. **How can I talk about my credentials while sharing what the work is about without sounding arrogant?**
   Keep your focus on why you have set up your site. If your reason is to promote yourself or your books, then you have to present posts that your followers will want to read and come back to view more. How?

   - **Involve Others**. Engage the reader. Make them active participants by inviting contributions; involve a guest blogger; start contests or projects.

- **Foster Relationships.** Readers need to feel like they belong. Generating a sense of community will build trust. It takes time. Loyalty doesn't happen over night.

- **Keep your selling voice out.** Through many posts, your audience will become friends. After a while, they will want to know more about you. They will want to help you just as you have helped them. Now sprinkle in more about what you are promoting.

Jo-Anne's 7 Tips on How To Post

1. Ask a question.
2. Share a quote or anecdote.
3. Stick with the content.
4. Pick out keywords or phrases and use them frequently.
5. Use subheadings so the reader can scan.
6. Create strong post titles.
7. Promote your site through online networks.

A WIN-WIN SITUATION

You can *conquer all obstacles* if you take one step at a time. You have learned strategies to **build an author platform, increase traffic through promotion**, and **how to post your content to keep your audience**. Break down each point and you will discover that YOU can create the site yourself AND enjoy the process.

First, treat your post like a rough draft. Write—what you do best—and don't worry about all the technicalities. Second, go back and edit. Finally, revise your post to make sure it meets the requirements you have been reading. Don't be afraid to use trial and error. Shout your fears away!

Think of writing your posts as learning the craft. Sometimes you are better off jumping into the deep end and trusting your instincts and expertise. You will resurface, float, and find dry land.

With time, your posts will become stronger, you will activate more followers, and you will really enjoy the writing itself. Establishing a site is a win-win situation. Not only will you be promoting your work, you will open the doors to greater opportunities. Nothing is better than meeting wonderful people you can call your friends.

Remember ... YOU can *conquer all obstacles*.

Podcasting: Promoting through BlogTalkRadio

*R*eady to increase traffic back to your site? Don't let your author profile and book just sit there. Now is the time to feature you, as the author, and your book.

Let's stir up those webcrawlers. They love to snag media in a variety of forms. This will boost your name even higher in the search engines (Google, Yahoo, MSN, etc.).

By hosting your own show through BlogTalkRadio, you can create FREE radio podcasts and syndicate your show to thousands of listeners through Facebook, Twitter, MySpace, etc. By copying, pasting and saving the widget of your show(s) on your blog, your specific followers and visitors can now simply click and listen right from your site.

Have you been asked to be a guest on a show?

If you have been asked to be a guest on a show, go for it! Agreeing to be interviewed will create a buzz that will generate massive exposure for you and your book.

Promoting your guest spot through your site and syndicating the broadcast throughout social media networks will increase traffic back to your site. That is FREE promotion!

It's simple. All you need is a computer with an Internet connection and a phone. The phone is necessary if you want to host a show or interact with hosts and/or guests.

All you have to do is:

1. **Register.**

2. **Download iTunes** (to save shows)

Are you researching new material for your book or post?

Through BlogTalkRadio, you can listen to recordings of shows that you missed in your subject of interest. Or download a show, then listen at a time that best suits you.

Perhaps you prefer a personal encounter on the subject of your choice. BlogTalkRadio allows participants to listen to "live" programs and participate through computer chat or call-in.

Now, talk about interactive!

You can *conquer all obstacles* by taking this easy step. Register for BlogTalkRadio(.com), and roam the site. Click on all the tabs. Check out the BlogTalkRadio Learning Center and hone in on the FAQs.

Start today ... you have nothing to lose and a lot to gain.

By hosting your own show through BlogTalkRadio, you can create FREE radio podcasts and syndicate your show to thousands of listeners.

Climbing To the Top: Search Engines

To conquer all obstacles and get your site climbing higher in those search engines, you must be prepared to do some work. Sure, establishing a readership so those hits grow in number is important, but now you will have to convince the webcrawlers.

How do I optimize my site from a search engine's perspective?

Register your site on Google, Yahoo, and MSN. Approximate Market Share: Google 63%, Yahoo 20%, Microsoft 9%, Ask 5%, AOL 4%.

Submit your website URL (only the main home page) to the top three search engines:

Google: http://www.google.com/addurl/?continue=/addurl
Yahoo: http://search.yahoo.com/info/submit.html
MSN: http://search.msn.com/docs/submit.aspx

Google actually says it is not necessary to submit your site because they will find you! They find you primarily through links from other sites. However, if links from other sites are in short supply, be sure to submit your site.

Once is enough, but please have your site finished and polished before submitting it.

Climbing up the search engine rankings takes time. Results are not going to happen over night.

"In my experience, it is not until a blog is 6 to 12 months old that it really begins to grow in its authority in Google."

—ProBlogger, *How to Grow Your Blog to the Next Level With SEO*

Register the site with "LinkReferral.com" or "Socialize It." Link these tag mechanisms by pasting their link on your page or site. For example, if you want your selling page to be the focus, make sure you place their symbol and links on that specific page. If you look on my PremiumPromotions.biz site, you will see the buttons placed in the widgets on the side bar and bottom of the main page. After the site is registered and you've linked sites, click on the buttons and tag your site using as many mechanisms as possible (Digg, StumbleUpon, Bookmark, etc.). Don't forget to include the tags. Bold the keywords, add them to heading tags and images.

Add more links. With high quality content, the traffic to your site will increase.

> *Soon others will make contact to link their blog with yours!*

Check out their site first. Go with your gut reactions. It doesn't hurt to reach out to others and request linkage. By accumulating links on similar niches, the keywords tagged will be emphasized and the speed to climb the up the ladder in the ranking process will increase.

Keep track of your stats. Analyze where the traffic is centralizing. Increase the internal links to these pages by adding extra links to the page. Include and highlight some of these pages in your sidebar or bottom of your posts. Again, do not forget to link the topic so your readers will simply navigate back to the high traffic topic. Do not delete these pingbacks; instead, highlight and apply them to your site. You may even decide to publish another post on the similar topic of interest.

You can *conquer all obstacles* by taking the time to manipulate the search engines to increase the ranking stats of your site. With more traffic heading to your site where your books are for sale, your chances of success will increase to greater sales.

Turn First Impressions Into Loyal Followers

*I*t can be a challenge to get your first time visitors to return to your blog/website, but it doesn't have to be. *Conquer all obstacles* by evaluating your site with the following checklist:

- ☐ **Make the subscribe button accessible.** Top side widget, label with clear instructions.
- ☐ **Occasionally remind your readers to subscribe.** Don't assume anything.
- ☐ **Produce an attractive blog/website design.** Make your site reader friendly—KISS.
- ☐ **Add personality, and engage your readers.** Use informal language, add pictures, invite viewers to contribute to the discussion. They will want to journey with you.
- ☐ **Revisit stats and analyze data.** What topics/posts have generated the most traffic? Capitalize on strengths.
- ☐ **Promote on social media sites.** "Connect with Jo-Anne," then list sites you belong to. Your viewers can follow you (i.e., FaceBook, GoodReads, MySpace, Gather.com, etc.).
- ☐ **Link to past posts.** New followers will appreciate being able to find what they have missed.
- ☐ **Give.** Readers are searching for answers, so give them what they want.
- ☐ **Be consistent.** Have a regular schedule, and keep the same formats in your post.
- ☐ **Find key players.** Encourage friendships. Opportunities will pop up.
- ☐ **Post great content and keep it fresh.** Engage your readers. Form a sense of community where readers feel they belong.

Tip #6 Social networking

Marketing and Promotions: Top 3

It should be no surprise that I love to read. This is an impossible expectation to lay on myself, but there are times when I simply cannot keep my eyes open any longer. Darn it, I really wanted to finish what I started reading.

Do you ever feel frustrated when there is not enough time in the day to finish everything you wanted to read?

To gain knowledge about today's rapidly changing technology, I try to read as many informative blogs as possible in my niche, marketing and promoting.

> *"I keep open an information page from Word where I add interesting links I have found and facts that will be useful."*
>
> —Jo-Anne Vandermeulen

What do I do with that page full of links and facts?

- I Twitter to my fellow writers so they can benefit. You can follow me at: http://www.twitter.com/conquerall

- I send them to my working partner, Brian Knight, and my editor/publisher, Nancy Williams, so we can remain on the same page and generate some very interesting discussions.

- I create the post for my "Conquer All Obstacles" blog. As part of this, I choose three sites/links to highlight. An example of these follows.

Interesting Links and Facts

1. **MARKETING TIPS FOR AUTHORS: TOP TEN WAYS AUTHORS CAN USE TWITTER | Dana Lynn Smith**
   http://blog.marketingtipsforauthors.com/2009/05/top-ten-ways-authors-can-use-twitter.html

   - **Share information and gain respect.** Become an expert in your field.
   - **Develop friendships.** Meet potential customers (readers) and stay in touch.
   - **Increase knowledge.** Today's news.
   - **Network.** Opportunities and partnerships may develop.
   - **Promote.** Announce happenings (book signings, etc.).
   - **Gain visibility** by holding contests.
   - **Resource support group.** Just ask ... The numbers of those who will follow through and help is amazing.
   - **Assist others.** Pay-it-forward—a win-win.
   - **Promote you and your book.** CAUTION: Use small doses to be affective.
   - **Stay in touch by cell phone.** Distance is no obstacle.

2. **WHEN IS THE TIPPING POINT FOR AN AUTHOR TO GO DIGITAL? | The Creative Penn**   http://bit.ly/qg7Ro

   - **Free or Cheap Digital Options:** Having a printed/digital book online is now possible.
   - **Load a Word document** for free and see it on Amazon.com to increase exposure through distributors. (Lulu.com)
   - **POD:** Sell your books without bulk in stock and no upfront cost.
   - **E-books:** Upload into free websites so others can download. (smashwords.com)
   - **Kindle DTP:** Thousands can access your book. Massive increase in website traffic.
   - **Podcasts:** Free audio software for a larger target audience. Meet people in the multi-media area.

3. **AMAZON'S KINDLE: ISSUES FOR BOOK PUBLISHERS, PRICING OPTIONS FOR E-BOOKS | By P. Olson & B. N. Anand | Book Business**
http://www.bookbusinessmag.com/article/amazons-kindle-has-raised-issues-book-publishers-such-appropriate-pricing-options-e-books-407856.html

- Kindle will dramatically change the way we purchase and read our books. Instant information is at our fingertips through wireless capabilities. There is even a potential for interaction. Portal information will be easily accessible for the reader. Readers will be able to feel a part of the author's community and their story.
- There is nothing wrong with a little more competition. More distributors are a good thing for authors. The author will have more control, forcing Amazon to stay on their toes. The results should be quite promising.
- The author should see a larger slice of the pie and gain a higher percentage of the profit.
- The future holds much promise for authors. They will be able to *conquer all obstacles* as technology for books advances.

Twusted Twitter Twools and Twips

Why is everyone talking about Twitter? Is this just a phase or will this be the next form of interaction to replace our blogs?

Today, many media social networkers are *twalking* or *twyping* with a form of speech impediment. But this is no speech impediment ... this is the new world of Twitter.

Twitter [twitter.com] is a VERY popular FREE micro-social network, a service for friends, family, and co-workers to communicate and stay connected through the exchange of quick, frequent messages (no longer than 140 characters).

Twusted Twitter Twools

There are many tools for Twitter users today, and more are surfacing all the time. The tools that prove to be more valuable will depend on the user's needs and purposes for Tweeting. Again, if you want to *conquer all obstacles* (just like blogging), you must ask yourself ...

WHY AM I TWEETING?

If you are trying to build an author platform, target an audience, and generate traffic back to your site where your books are sold, then the following are a few tools that you cannot afford to be without:

- **Twaitter** – Twitter tool to schedule reoccurring tweets. Free. http://www.twaitter.com/
- **Tweetbeep** – Discover what others are Twitting about that has to do with you ... Twitter Alerts – http://tweetbeep.com/
- **Bit.ly** – Allows users to shorten, share, and track links (URLs). Reducing the URL length makes sharing easier. http://bit.ly/pages/about/

SITES FOR WRITERS WHO TWEET

- **Twitter Directory** – A must have "Writer's List" ... if you Twitter, this list is valuable: http://www.highspotinc.com/blog/2008/12/a-directory-of-book-trade-people-on-twitter/
- **Marketing Tips For Authors:** "Top Ten Ways Authors Can Use Twitter," by Dana Lynn Smith: http://blog.marketingtipsforauthors.com/2009/05/top-ten-ways-authors-can-use-twitter.html

TWITTER TIPS

On your Twitter profile page:

1. **Bio** – Most followers will read the one-line bio under "SETTINGS." Rather than sending them to the home page profile, include a direct link to your personal profile page. *Example:* View Profile of JoVan@ppromotionals – Internet Promo Manager: http://joconquerobstacles.com/2009/03/19/a-little-bit-more-about-jo-anne-vandermeulen/

2. **Follow-up** – Investigate your followers. Send them a direct message, such as:
   TY for following. I'm a Sask. gal. Run my own Internet Promo business at: http://bit.ly/6aCh3 and a personal blog at: http://bit.ly/pGGZX

3. **Feeds** – A simple feed that allows your Twitter post to automatically show up on your blog or website. Click on "SETTINGS," scroll down to "MORE INFO URL" and click on the "BLUE LINK – YOU CAN ALSO ADD TWITTER TO YOUR SITE HERE," and just follow the steps.

4. **Promote** – Advertise your Twitter link everywhere you can. Include your Twitter link to your signature. Add comments on Twitter discussions, and leave a direct message with others who are following you.

A WRITER MUST *CONQUER ALL OBSTACLES*

- Build an author platform that stands out from the rest.
- Target an audience suited to your niche or genre.
- Generate traffic (friends/fans) back to your site.
- Display a fabulous site highlighting you and your books. (Do not forget the visible button to purchase your book).

Note: *Take heed to the above tools, sites, and tips. When you continuously add a "w" after the "t" you will know you've been Tweeting a tad too long.*

How To Sell Books

Use Your Site and Internet Social Media to Present Your Book

Congratulations! The buzz is happening. You have managed to *conquer all obstacles* by accomplishing these gigantic first steps in marketing your book(s):

- [ ] **You have successfully targeted your reading audience** by reaching out and interacting with other people who would be more inclined to purchase the book or material you have to offer.
- [ ] **The number of your followers has increased, and your name is exposed.** More and more people are requesting your friendship in all the social media sites.
- [ ] **You have established strong relationships.** These followers are becoming your fans.
- [ ] **Your blog/website is filled with valuable content and is linked to high traffic sites. It has an attractive appeal that draws people in.** Visitors are leaving comments on your site. Checking out the Feedburner and Google Analytics stats, you see peaks indicating that hits and subscribers are increasing.
- [ ] **Your name and the title of your book are showing up on the first page of the Google search engine.** You are carefully selecting tags, or keywords, with all your posts. The webcrawlers are picking you up and taking you to the top. No longer do your potential customers have to scroll through several pages of search results to find you. (Let's face it, they probably wouldn't anyway.)

If you can honestly check off the points listed above, you can accept a grand sense of accomplishment. Reward yourself! *(Wine and chocolate work well for me.)*

Creating a buzz is a major accomplishment. It takes a lot of time and effort to achieve a buzz and create exposure in the massively competitive realm of the Internet. Building an author platform is no simple feat.

But don't stop now. *(Okay, take a break with your wine and chocolate.)* You have another obstacle to conquer ...

> *There is a VERY important step you must accomplish to market your books successfully. You must ...*
> **SELL YOUR BOOKS!**

Let's put our feet in our potential customers' shoes. They call us by our first name. They know where we and our books are located in cyberspace, and they trust what we have to say. Forty percent (40%) of them would probably purchase our books in an instant. As long as our Buy Now buttons are displayed and the process is simple, they will click, and a sale happens. But what about the other sixty percent of our fans?

These followers may hesitate just prior to pushing that Buy Now button. Perhaps they have been burned by a non-ethical person luring them into a purchasing situation. Sales people are bred to be very good at what they do.

It is up to us to provide the proof that we are legitimate by supplying a sample of what our buyers will receive.

Think of the last time you went into a bookstore. Unless a friend recommended a title, or you heard it was on the best seller list, you would need to check out an unknown author or book title before purchasing. You probably flipped it over and read the back. Maybe you even opened the cover and read the first page or two before deciding the book was good enough to purchase.

As authors marketing our books online, we can provide the "taste sample" they need. If our book has not hit the best seller list and our viewer has never heard of us or our books, we can *conquer all obstacles* by presenting the first few pages or even a chapter of our book right on our site where our platform is located.

> ***It is vital that you supply a sample of your writing for your potential customers to read.***

Along with your book cover, purchase button, short synopsis, reviews, interviews, and that wonderful content you have been supplying, it is vital that you supply a sample of your writing for your potential customers to read.

What if I told you that it is possible for you to supply an attractive display right on your site? Picture your fan entering your site, physically opening the cover of your book, flipping each page, and reading your story.

This amazing method is not entirely new. Here are a few examples of distributors using this tool:

- **Harper Collins**—Has a site for e-books. *"Browse Inside – Try Before You Buy."*

- **Amazon**—Had pioneered this tactic in 2003 by *"Offering Samples."*

- **Random House, Inc.**—By clicking on a binoculars icon, the reader can *"Browse and Search"* within the text of the chosen book.

These distributors are keeping up with the dramatic changes in society by taking advantage of the strong market expansion of Internet purchasing and are now meeting the needs of all types of customers.

Harper Collins had a similar experience with sales. Harper Collins reported print sales increases of 30% and 250% for specific titles using their Browse Inside functionality.

Amazon, who pioneered offering samples on a large scale in 2003, reported about 9% increase in print sales across 120,000 titles in 5 days after the search inside capability was available on their site.

These companies have come to realize that targeting markets is a better promotional strategy than broadcasting the old fashioned advertising way, and you can, too.

A book widget called **BookBuzzr** is now available at www.freado.com. It is a portable author website that extracts book information supplied by the author and makes your content accessible on many social media sites—FaceBook, Blogs, MySpace, LinkedIn, etc. Now you can upload your pages, and your cover will be displayed on several of your personal profiles, including your web/blogsite, for your viewers to flip the pages and read.

Just think of the exposure!

Fans and acquaintances will be able to sample your book by just clicking on the cover image. Even if your personal site is not getting the traffic you would like, others will soon discover your book through these massive traffic media sites.

BookBuzzr is FREE and will give you the exposure that you deserve. Try it.

> ***You can* conquer all obstacles *and successfully market and sell your book.***

Marketing and promoting

No More Fear

One of my biggest fears in life is getting lost. My palms are sweaty just thinking about it. Having no sense of direction is not only a daunting fear for many writers, they also feel completely lost. This is a reality.

But fear no more. To *conquer all obstacles* is to have direction. I will show you easy steps for promoting yourself and your books. It requires that you **devise a specific plan** and **discover your balance**.

It is good to plan, but don't plan the outcome. That will only set up expectations. Like writing, enjoy the process, and the product is a bonus. Write it down. Don't keep it all in your head. Visual succession, some sort of measurement of progression, is proven to boost moral. It will give you an enlightened sense of completion.

Answer the five "Ws," and your plan is set in motion.

The 5-W Marketing Plan:
Who, What, When, Where and (we know) Why

WHO?	Who is your audience, those interested in your book(s)?
WHAT?	What services will generate the most exposure?
WHEN?	When will you contact your waiting fans and followers?
WHERE?	Where will you display your profile and book(s)?
WHY?	We know why … to sell your book(s)!

To learn more, please check out: Premium Promotional Services *You Write – We Promote*
http://www.premiumpromotions.biz

Too many of us want to jump to the "Where" in the marketing plan. We want to know where to go before addressing the Who, What, and When.

A marketing plan is not the place to take shortcuts. Skipping steps will only result in confusion or wasted time marketing in the wrong place. Discover a balance.

Where to promote will come automatically after you have gone through the progressive steps of planning and completing the Who, What, and When.

WHO?

Who is your audience, those interested in your book(s)?

- Search for followers in a variety of areas, such as Social Media networks, e.g., Facebook, Goodreads, Red Room, Gather.com, AuthorsDen, LinkedIn, ShoutLife.
- Network in many different groups. Join discussions and leave your brand/signature.
- Promote locally at book signings, presentations, etc., and reach out to the Internet.
- Vary your presentation techniques to fit the needs of each individual. Who you are chatting with will determine the formality of the conversation.

WHAT?

What services will generate the most exposure?

- Meet the needs of your viewers by selecting as many services as possible: Author Platforms, Book Reviews, Author Interviews, Virtual Tours, Blog/Website Redesign.
- Sprinkle these service throughout the social networks in a press release format.
- Introduce your book soon after introducing yourself. (Many viewers will already be asking about it.) Don't push the sale yet. Give the viewers a chance to be hooked.
- Sprinkle in a little more service. No ... don't push yet.

WHEN?

When will you contact your waiting fans and followers?
- Schedule your day by dividing the clock. Keep track of how you spend your time, and then evaluate. Did you finish what you planned? If the answer is no, ask yourself why?
- The next day, try rearranging your priorities. What you did not complete yesterday may fit in today.

WHERE?

Where will you display your profile and book(s)?
- After you identify *Who* your target audience is; *What* services you are sprinkling into the market; and *When*, the amount of time will be allotted to each group; the *Where* is simple.

WHY?

We know why ... to sell your book(s)!
Now you can sell your book. Set the hook and reel in your fans. Push hard, be strong, and don't hold anything back.

You can *conquer all obstacles* by following a plan of action—a marketing plan of the 5-Ws. The secret to selling your book is knowing *who* to address, *what* services or tactics work, *when* to set the hook and start reeling in the fans, and *where* all the action takes place. No one likes a pushy salesperson; nor do they like to be left in limbo. It is up to you to find that balance.

Trust your instincts by really listening to your viewers.

Give your fans what they want—your book. Wow! It is a win-win situation. I like that, and look ... my palms are dry.

Learn From the Best

Market Yourself Hard …

"Good stories are not about one topic, but explore numerous threads. And no radio or TV program wants to invite you on to re-tell your novel. So instead of focusing on the story, most fiction writers find they have to focus on the author or the genre. In other words, you and your voice become the focus of your marketing. This is why it's essential that a novelist has a clear style. Think of the marketing of successful novelists —it's not always the story that is the focus but the fact that there is another great book from John Grisham or Elizabeth George or Janet Evanovich. (Sometimes the focus is a bit more on the genre—the publisher wants readers to know this is an Amish story, or a techno-thriller, or a cross-cultural adventure story. But that's much less frequent.) Looking at today's market, what's the lesson? Discover your voice. Write a great novel. Market yourself hard."

—**Chip MacGregor,** *Literary Agent*
chipmacgregor.typepad.com/main/

Promote, Pronounce, and Present …

PROMOTE:
- Promote yourself and your book before the launch date.

PRONOUNCE:
- Communicate. Let your readers know they can pre-order.
- Activate strategies to contact book clubs. Think of low cost and more effective ways to generate sales.

PRESENT:
- Put yourself out there. Discussion groups generate thinking among members with common interests.
- Readers play an active part in getting to know you by following the conversations.

- Generate strands of different book clubs. That equals more followers for the author.
- Be prepared to actively participate. Relax and enjoy.

Appearance, Attitude, Activate ...

APPEARANCE:
- Dress professionally during any public appearance—book signings, interviews, etc. Wear black/white or blue/white and no dangling jewelry. (I know, guys, this is a given.)

ATTITUDE:
- Understand how the industry works. Bookshelves are only so big. Your book may not be in every bookstore, and that is okay.

ACTIVATE:
- Encourage the audience to look at your book by telling them they can read the first chapter and back cover.
- Physically hand them the book.
- Watch your body language and don't force.
- Create excitement by greeting the shopper and smiling.
- Wait until they have finished reading before chatting.
- Hand out bookmarks to others as they pass. Give them a useful bookmark with colorful cover pictures and text that intrigues. And of course, have your website URL printed on it.
- Ask questions. Example: "Are you looking for Christmas gift ideas or something good to read?"

Market, Market, Market ...

MARKET:
- Identify and really know your target audience (age, gender, and interest).
- Think outside the box to discover strategies (local press releases, media interviews, blogging, and visitations). Be

bold, daring, and creative. Afterwards, evaluate which strategies are working best and which are not working.
- Search and discover, hook, and then retain your followers.

> *"Risk! Risk anything! Care no more for the opinions of others, for those voices. Do the hardest thing on earth for you. Act for yourself. Face the truth."*
> —Katherine Mansfield

Have faith. You can *conquer all obstacles*. Just use a little common sense, listen and learn from the experience of others. Bask in the glory by knowing you are a truly valuable person with something to say, and you are doing your best.

> *"I see the notion of talent as quite irrelevant. I see instead perseverance, application, industry, assiduity, will, will, will, desire, desire, desire."*
> —Gordon Lish

Scams: Beware of the Swarming Sharks

*T*rust takes a long time to gain and only a second to lose. I know—I've been burned. Thankfully, I turned to the Internet and Googled myself silly. While on the World Wide Web (www), I discovered there are many supportive authors who are in the same boat.

> **What a wonderful feeling to belong to a community of caring people.**

Unfortunately, there are many who have not been so lucky. They have become victims of scammers. Some have lost thousands of dollars and had their dream of publishing and selling their "baby" crushed.

In my prior profession, I was often accused of being too compassionate. Yes, I took my work home with me. I let the sorrow of others absorb through my skin and sink deeply into my veins. I felt compelled to defend my friends. As a teacher, I wanted to take many of my students home with me; I knew their homes were not good for them. Gosh, it's sad!

Today, I feel the same. I want to help defend my fellow writers. An invisible force is compelling me to warn of the sharks swarming just below the surface, ready to go for the kill. Don't be their next meal.

WARNING SIGNS: BEWARE THE SHARKS!

Let's say you have decided that you would rather write and leave the business of promoting to someone who has the time, knowledge, and ability to promote you and your books. I cannot say I blame you. Promoting is a full time job. And if you are anything like me, having trouble shifting from the art or craft of writing (which is produced from the right hemisphere of the brain) to the business of selling (from the left hemisphere of the brain), you may not have any other choice. You will have to either hire someone, or you will have to stop writing and begin selling.

Before you decide to hire someone to provide promotional services of any kind, do your homework. Ask for referrals from past clients. Watch for any false or misleading phrases.

DO NOT BE FRESH BAIT FOR THESE PHRASES:

- *"We can guarantee book sales."*

   No one can guarantee to sell your book! There are too many variables that determine success. Too many circumstances can erupt that are out of the marketer's control.

   Example: Today's dictating market to favorite genres—Romance is a huge selling genre; Westerns are in a slight slump.

   Example: A completed product or manuscript is subjective in the eyes of others. Is your writing favorable to the majority of an audience? Remember, what you like doesn't dictate what everyone else will like. Even a title can sometimes make or break a few sales.

   Example: The economic condition can cause market fluctuations.

> **Fact:** *Creating an author platform, targeting the right audience, building relationships with readers, generating traffic to the site where your book is sold will increase the chances of the successful sale of your book.*

No matter what anyone does, there are still no guarantees in regard to book sales, and no promotional manager or marketer should ever tell you otherwise.

- *"We can get you into the top search engines."*
  This is a misleading statement. There are many active webcrawlers that constantly hoist new material up and down within seconds.

> **Fact:** *Establishing internal and external links will activate webcrawlers to raise your ranks in the search engines, but to state that you and your books will be placed at the top is highly unlikely.*

Even if you are at the top of the search engines, you will most likely only be there for a second, and then the shift continues.

- *"We can get you media exposure now."*
  Wrong! Promotion takes time. Building a platform takes time. There is too much competition out there. A promotional manager has to create an author profile that stands out from the rest, draws the attention of the viewers, establishes a trusting relationship with followers, then navigates the fans to the purchase button. Believe me ... this does not happen over night. Selling a book takes a lot of hard work and even a little luck.

> **Fact:** *Marketing takes time, dedication, and complete commitment.*

No matter how good something sounds, take a step back and draw a deep breath. Take time to research and inquire.

Conquer all obstacles, and drive away the predators by not becoming shark bait. Sharks will not stick around if there is no prey.

Leave the Promoting to Someone Else

You have read the book. You have considered the steps necessary to market and promote yourself and your book, and you have decided it's not for you. You would rather hire a professional to do the marketing and promoting so you can do what you love best: write.

Jo-Anne Vandermeulen's **Premium Promotional Services** could be your answer. The following interview will answer a lot of your questions when making the promotional decision.

An Interview With Jo LINSDELL

PROMO DAY: PREMIUM PROMOTIONAL SERVICES

What is Premium Promotional Services?

Premium Promotional Services (PPS) is a professional business created to help writers. We aggressively market the author and their books through individual or a combination of promotional services. Premium Promotional Services provides ALL the author's promotional needs—massive exposure guaranteed.

We custom design a promotional package that best suits each client's needs. At PPS, we provide author advertising, book title promotions, Site creation, special author Fan pages, existing site redesign, and a book video. *You Write – We Promote* at Premium Promotional Services.

When did you launch Premium Promotional Services?

With the vision 'to help writers' existing for a long time, we officially opened Premium Promotional Services cyber-doors March 2, 2009.

Why did you start Premium Promotional Services?

By 2008, I had two polished novels ready to be published. Through nearly a hundred workshops, a few pitching sessions with editors, submission responses from nearly a thousand agents, I soon discovered they all voiced the same concern ... "How are you going to promote yourself? Please provide me with information about your author platform." My first response was: "What? You mean I can't just write?" There was nowhere to turn. All doors remained shut.

I set forth to research the area of promotion. I learned I needed to target an audience, build friendships through networks, and provide my followers with a platform they loved. I started my first blog, Jo-Anne Vandermeulen *"Conquer All Obstacles,"* providing assistance to fellow writers. After a few posts, the comments started pouring in.

The first door flew open ...

I immediately discovered my niche. Authors from all over the world cried help, requesting promotional services. Through many hours of studying the promotional business and connecting with professionals, I produced templates for author platforms, explored strategies to target an audience, and generated a buzz of massive activity. Through my journey, I discovered techniques to climb to the top of the world wide search engines. Suddenly, I was performing my services to over a BILLION viewers on the Internet. No longer was I invisible. I had done it! The large number of hits, responses, and dashboard stats proved that I had successfully promoted myself.

The second door flew open ...

On March 2, 2009, with the help of my business partner, Brian Knight, Premium Promotional Services launched into production—a writer's solution to all their promotional and marketing needs. Through my personal blog, Conquer All Obstacles, and the business blog, Premium Promotional Services, there is no better way to share the knowledge I have gained to help my fellow writers. I can successfully provide a requested service while they can continue to write.

What services does Premium Promotional Services offer?
- Site Creation
- Author Advertising
- Special Author Fan Pages
- Site Redesign
- Book Title Promotion
- Book Video

Where can people find out more about Premium Promotional Services?

You can find more about Premium Promotional Services through our website: http://www.premiumpromotions.biz

If you have any further questions, please feel free to contact us through the website or in person.

Jo-Anne Vandermeulen: jo@ppromotionals.net
Brian Knight: brian@ppromotionals.net

Is there anything else you'd like to add?
Our goal at Premium Promotional Services is to market the author and their book(s) using effective and powerful promotional tactics. With the Internet promotional expertise to optimize search engines and generate streams of readers, the author's name and book(s) will surface to the top.

Brian and I will provide the vehicle with the author behind the wheel. At Premium Promotional Services "You Write – We Promote."

Thank you to Jo Linsdell, creator and manager of Authors and Writers, for hosting this interview.

Exposure, Exposure, Exposure!

Are you searching for more exposure for your book(s)? Exposure is a must in successfully promoting your book(s).

If you have not sold the rights to your book to a major publisher or signed an exclusive distribution package, then you are free to list your book(s) with as many distribution sites as you choose.

> *"More power to the author to list their books with as many distributors as possible."*

My business partner, Brian Knight, has opened a cyber bookstore on our **Premium Promotional Services** website: www.premiumpromotions.biz

Are you interested in having a reputable professional promotional company list your book right on their site? The traffic flow going to the Premium Promotional Services (PPS) site is huge!

With each new book that is added to the PPS Bookstore, we ping over 90 directories. It is properly indexed through social bookmarks. With each new book that is added, we activate the webcrawlers through internal and external links, creating optimal search engine ranks.

Take advantage of this FREE offer,* and list your book today. Adding new books to the PPS Bookstore generates more traffic, so spread the word to fellow authors. ACT TODAY and boost your book's visibility.

If you are interested in adopting another distributor for FREE, please leave a message in the Comments section on the PPS site at: www.premiumpromotions.biz

---

*NOTE: Your book must be listed with Amazon to take advantage of this FREE offer.

BOOK DISTRIBUTORS

Want to gain more exposure? Here is a list of sites where you can register your book, submit your author platform, a book synopsis with book covers, and add reviews. Don't forget to highlight the site where your books are sold.

- Librarything
- Goodreads
- Shelfari
- Anobii
- Authorsden
- NothingBinding
- Weread
- Authortree
- Internet Authors Network – http://www.xenite.org/internet_authors/announcebooks.html
- Authonomy
- Facebook
- Red Room
- Gather.com
- LinkedIn
- Blogged.com
- ShoutLife
- Twitter
- Goodreads
- Book Marketing Network
- Book Blog (Ning)
- WinterFace
- www.polkadotbanner.com – Good new site, not yet registered.
- www.booktour.com
- Connectviabooks
- www.axisavenue.com – Excellent site to add profile and books and distributers.

For maximum exposure, have your publisher list your books with the following distributors:

- Premium Promotional Services
- Amazon.com
- Barnes & Noble
- Amazon.co.uk
- Buy.com
- WHSmith
- Author House
- Yahoo Books
- Borders.com (UK site)
- Booksamillion

A couple of thoughts from the e-book scene. One site to add is: http://www.Smashwords.com

Also, don't forget about Amazon's digital text platform that lets you upload your book as a Kindle book. That address is: https://dtp.amazon.com/

In Canada, most libraries purchase their books through library services, and the best way I have found to get into libraries here is to contact these library service companies directly. If you offer them a sufficient discount on your book, they will include it in their mailouts to libraries. This may be a small but untapped market for writers in the USA.

http://www.lsc.on.ca/

They service the province of Ontario, which has one-third of the Canadian population, and are open to self-published works as long as the discount is good.

In Canada, authors also get paid a small amount based on the number of books they have in libraries. It is not very much, but you get paid for each title. The whole idea is to compensate the author somewhat for lost sales since many people will read the book for free instead of buying it.

If you are a Canadian, then Google "Public Lending Rights." You will find that there is a window in February/March to submit ISBNs that match their criteria, which includes all novels. They will pick 25 Canadian libraries, I presume at random, and look for your books. I think they say that the average payment made to authors each year is about $600.00, but they do pay on titles for fifteen years from the publication date.

Why not donate a copy of your book to a local library? ask them to "catalogue" it, and that will get it into the system. If it is available through their distributor, other libraries can pick it up if they want to. If you donate a copy of each of your books to a local library, it may open opportunities for invitational talks and signings.

OTHER RESOURCES

- Excellent writing database from Nathan Bransford, Literary Agent: http://blog.nathanbransford.com/

- Amazon Kindle – issues for book publishers, pricing options for e-books. Book Business: http://bit.ly/Zih4B

- Where I Write – photos of writer workspaces: http://www.whereiwrite.org/

- Excellent Marketing Advice Database for Writers: Jo-Anne Vandermeulen "Conquer All Obstacles" http://bit.ly/vXrQc

You can conquer all obstacles to get your book sold!

- Create massive exposure for you and your book.
- Build an author platform that stands out from the rest.
- Target an audience suited to your niche or genre.
- Blog! Blog! Blog!
- Generate traffic (friends/fans) back to your site.
- Develop a social networking community to share and support.

Finally, be sure to display a fabulous site that highlights you and your books. Be sure to include a compelling **Buy Now** button.

Conquer All Obstacles!

Interviews with Jo-Anne

An Interview With SHARON BALL

Sharon Ball writes upbeat posts in a blog called, "A Break From The Norm." The following is an interview she conducted with Jo-Anne Vandermeulen. Check out her blog and be prepared to be fully entertained.

Enjoy the interview.

A prolific writer of romantic fiction, Jo-Anne Vandermeulen is also an Internet promotional manager for her business called Premium Promotional Services, *You Write – We Promote*. Bi-weekly, she posts on her personal blog, *Conquer All Obstacles,* FREE user-friendly articles for writers who want to learn more about marketing and promotional tactics. She recently earned Expert Author status on EzineArticles as her submissions have been accepted for publication.

Can you share with us a few tips for marketing books and other products using the internet?
- Define your niche. Territorialize Your Position, and Intensify Your Niche.
  http://gr5mom2.wordpress.com/2009/03/26/defining-your-niche/
- Develop strategies to stand out from the rest – Meet The Needs Of Your Viewers.   http://gr5mom2.wordpress.com/2009/03/24/how-can-a-writer-stand-out-from-the-rest/
- Turn first impressions into loyal followers – It can be a challenge to get your first time visitors to return to your

blog/website, but it doesn't have to be.
http://gr5mom2.wordpress.com/2009/03/12/turning-first-impressions-into-loyal-followers/
- Create a buzz – I want to promote myself, show the world my writing/published books, but where do I start?
http://gr5mom2.wordpress.com/2009/03/06/creating-a-buzzzzzz/
- Direct traffic
http://gr5mom2.wordpress.com/2009/02/25/field-guide-to-blogging/
- Blog the right way – Is there a correct way to blog?
http://gr5mom2.wordpress.com/2009/02/19/blog-the-right-way/
- Develop an attractive blog/website to generate traffic
http://gr5mom2.wordpress.com/2009/01/08/attractive-blogwebsite-generates-traffic/
- Climb to the top ranks in the Search Engines – How do I optimize my site in a search engine's perspective?
http://joconquerobstacles.com/2009/04/09/climbing-to-the-top-%E2%80%93-a-search-engine%E2%80%99s-perspective/
- Blog professionally – How do I create a blog that *conquers all obstacles* and stays out of the slush pile?
http://gr5mom2.wordpress.com/2009/04/16/professional-blogging/
- Produce a great post – "Blogging: A Delicious Post Devoured In One Bite"

How do you combine great needed content and infuse your post with perspective and background to make it real for the reader?
http://gr5mom2.wordpress.com/2009/04/21/blogging-a-delicious-post-devoured-in-one-bite/

Can you share with us a few tips for marketing books and other products using the internet?
- Create an attractive blog – Your blog will work as an interactive link to your main site where you sell your books.
- Faithfully, post interesting and interactive articles.
- Design an author platform that will stand out from the

rest and feature yourself on this blog.
- Link the purchase button/book cover on every page.
- Establish a stationary blog/website – Your site, where you sell your books, should be very user-friendly (simple navigation).
- Install webcrawlers – This technique will help to snag your site. Have internal and external links so your keywords will rank high in the search engines.
- Remind yourself that "marketing" is a business – Be professional and interact with your customers; yet, don't be too pushy, or you'll scare them away.
- Include strategies in your marketing plan – Develop a brand/signature, use tags, and network like crazy with your target audience.
- Join discussion groups and promote your site – Constantly promote your site to Internet social media networks like Goodreads, Facebook, Shoutlife, Authorsden, LinkedIn, LibraryThing, Shelfari, Ning.com, Gather.com, Red Room, Twitter, etc.

As someone experienced in Internet marketing and promotion, what are some of the biggest lessons you have learned that you wish someone would have told you when you first started in the business?
- It is a lot of work! I knew this when I opened Premium Promotional Services, but I underestimated the huge time commitment involved in promoting even one client.
- Technology is constantly changing, and these changes are occurring faster and faster all the time. To keep up with these rapid advancements, constant education must be a part of my routine. It's almost like going back to school and having to take a couple of hours of instruction every day just to keep afloat. I guess I needed to actually experience this fast pace before I could really relate. And now that I know, I just hold on and enjoy the ride.

- The Internet world is HUGE! The biggest lesson that I've learned from starting this business is the sense of community—how vast this writing world really is and the great people I've met in this new journey.

What advice would you give to someone who is new to blogging?
- KISS. Keep It Simple, Silly. Don't be afraid. Enjoy the creativity that grows naturally inside of you. If you have a problem, ask. There are so many of us who will jump at the chance to help. We are all in this together.
- If you don't know your niche, don't worry. Babble away; there are no wrong answers. Your audience will guide you … so listen. It takes time, so be patient.

What has your experience been with using various forms of social media like LinkedIn and Twitter to promote yourself and/or your service offerings?
- I connect weekly with a dozen social media networks. Each has its own audience and is an effective way to promote. You can never have too many friends.
- I view the stats on my profile. I have determined that the time and energy spent at each network is directly proportional to the number of hits or views. For example, when I began networking, I was on MySpace because it was quite popular. Now, it has died down and the new and upbeat place to hang out is ShoutLife. A promoter must be prepared to change and learn new areas. I find myself on the lookout all the time.

An Interview With NOUVEAUWRITER

ASK THE EXPERT: MARKETING SERVICES AND THEIR BENEFITS

NouveauWriter has interviewed Marketing Expert Jo-Anne Vandermeulen for insight on today's publishing and marketing situation and how authors can benefit from learning about this important step in their career.

How long have you been writing?
I've been writing since I could pick up a pencil. As a child, I wrote daily journals and pleaded with anyone who would exchange letters and be my pen pal. In high school, I fell in love with creative writing. The process, the product, or published work, was heaven. I fed off the positive responses of my listeners. I continued this writing into university and studied to become an educator with an English major. Teaching for twenty years allowed me to share my expertise and immerse myself further into my passion.

Due to an unforeseen illness, I moved from the classroom to a quiet living room. Luckily, I was able to take that devastation and turn it around as an opportunity. As of April 2006, I've been writing full time.

In your opinion, how has the publishing industry changed, and how has this affected authors?
Seventeen days after I started writing from the solitude of my living room, I had my first manuscript completed. (I guess the story had been in me for a long time.) I immediately targeted agents, feeling I would prosper more if I went through the traditional publishers in New York. Response was very good. The requested partial, and even full, manuscripts were submitted. But like most aspiring authors, I soon discovered I had a lot to learn. The real work started.

I took online workshops and read anything I could get my hands on. I networked with other authors, joined groups, attended writer conventions, and sent my novel to readers, editors, and judges in contests—anyone who would give me feedback.

At the same time, I produced a second novel. I tried going the same route in the publishing world, but this time, I noticed a huge difference. The acceptance of partials declined, and even though I was asked to submit a full manuscript, this too was quickly rejected.

Today, I feel the traditional publishers are not taking any risks. New aspiring authors have an even smaller chance of breaking into the tight traditional publishing world.

Looking at other publishing options, I am in the process of determining a new venture.

My published article in my *Conquer All Obstacles* blog, "Ruined Reputation Comes To A Halt," states publishing facts as of February 2009. I have come to accept that promotion is on the author's shoulders and, if we are going to make any money from our hard work, we will have to do it ourselves.

Thankfully, there are services such as Premium Promotional Services and plenty of support groups we can turn to for help. Unfortunately, this carves a huge groove out of our precious writing time. It is now more difficult for writers to pursue their passion to just write. They are having to squeeze into a business suit and perform marketing duties that are out of their comfort zone.

On a positive note, this new publishing venture puts the author into the driver's seat. We have control and will make more profit from our sales, compared with going through the traditional publishers.

"Ruined Reputation Comes To A Halt" states the percentage of how much is left for the author after the other disbursement of income to a book seller, publisher, agent, etc. This new avenue of publishing dictates very surprising results—more favorable in the hands of the author.

How important is marketing one's book today?

"Who Likes To Get Naked?" is an article I published on March 10, 2009, in my *Conquer All Obstacles* blog. Think of your published book sitting on the shelf or hanging in cyberspace—lonely and naked. Unless the author has the expertise and can take the time to market his or her books, this is what will likely happen. There is another alternative. The author can continue writing and purchase promotional services. Someone else will then be taking care of all their promotional needs.

Promoting your book is VERY important. Without exposing yourself to create an audience (trusted fans and followers), targeting possible consumers, and linking your viewers to the site that sells your books, your book will just sit there shivering. There are too many other books for people to buy. As an Internet Promotional Manager, I have learned tactics to lift an author and their books to the top of major search engines.

Now, the consumer doesn't have to search for you. Instead, the author will be visible—totally exposed, but fully dressed. And it is my job to make sure that this author and his or her books stand out and are unique from the rest by producing a professional author platform to fire out for over a BILLION Internet viewers. Talk about massive exposure!

How has the Internet changed marketing authors and their books?

Marketing and promotion have always been the success factor in selling books. Today, marketing is even more important. According to Peter Miller, Literary Manager with PMA Literary, *"We look for authors who not only are great writers but are willing to promote their work and who also understand the enormous SEA changes in the industry. It used to be 75% about how good the book was and 25% about the marketing but now it is 75% about the marketing and 25% how good the book is."*

When we consider marketing on the Internet, the doors just fly open.

Second quarter of 2008, the Census Bureau of the Department of Commerce stated that the total number of Internet users worldwide was 1,463,500,000 viewers with over 40,000 social media sites to hang out, 7 days a week, 24 hours a day. Need I say any more? Talk about exposure!

Do traditionally published authors have to promote like a self-published author?

Building an Author Platform and promotion should occur even before the author is published in either forms. Many authors are publishing articles in their blogs before they are officially published—an excellent way to promote themselves.

"According to Technorati, someone creates a new blog every 1.4 seconds," says Adam Brown, FreelanceSwitch Site.

In order for a writer to create a following, they must establish "friends." A form of trust has to happen between the writer and their future fans in the form of networking.

Networking, networking, networking is a must and is very time consuming, but the results are worth it. Success doesn't occur overnight—there is no instant gratification. Promotion takes a lot of time. Yet, it works like a snowball rolling down a snow covered hill.

Building an author platform before you are published is probably one of the most important marketing tactics you can create and later contribute to your success. Think of walking into a bookstore. Do you usually remember the title of the book or the author's name?

Donna Bagdasarian from Maria Carvainis Agency wrote: Is platform more important than it was maybe five years ago and if so, why? "Platform is crucial. To a publisher, a platform speaks to audience. So, first, you need the credentials. Second, you need to form some sort of grassroots following."

Even traditional publishers stress the importance of authors self-promoting. The authors must do a lot of the work themselves.

Tell us about your blog and your new service for authors.

My blog, *Conquer All Obstacles,* started as a way for me to find my niche in life. Sure I wanted to promote myself as an aspiring author, but, at the same time, I needed to see if there were other opportunities that God had planned for my life. Since I got sick, I've had to throw my hands up in the air and let Him take over. Not such a bad thing, really.

I developed my personal blog to share my knowledge with fellow writers. I love to learn—research things to death. And my teaching background makes blogging a natural way for me to educate others. Lately, my main category has focused around marketing and promoting, but scanning back through past posts, everything is there. From learning the craft of writing to my personal experiences being an aspiring author, the posts are written in a friendly, informal manner that allows followers to take knowledge and apply it to themselves.

My niche evolved in the past six months. I found myself focusing more and more on the promotional aspects of writing. Believe me, it wasn't because I wanted to—I dreaded it. The online courses spoke about how important it was for an aspiring author to market themselves and their books, but the information seemed way over my head and a lot of work I didn't think I could handle.

Surprisingly, the more I read, researched, and networked with fellow promoters, the more interested I became. The obsession took over, and I was swimming right in the thick of things, totally loving the challenging new information. Applying the information soon became even more of a thrill. I discovered techniques that actually worked and I gained instant success. Other authors began coming to me, asking for my promotional services ... "What services?"

March 2, 2009, was the launch date of Premium Promotional Services, a business to meet the needs and requested demands of writers. My partner, Brian Knight, who is an expert in specific services such as author interviews, book reviews, blog generation, author tours, and revising existing blogs/websites, joined me in my vision. Brian is just the right person to compliment my Premium Promotional Service.

Together, we have our hearts set on helping writers. We care. At Premium Promotional Services, *You Write – We Promote*. Now writers can leave ALL the promotional work to us, so they will have the time to write, to happily pursue their passion, to remain in their artistic outfit and leave the business suits to us.

I specifically provide an Author Advertising service. On a one-to-one basis, I work extremely hard and put hundreds of hours in promoting you and your books.

I have the knowledge to expose your site where your books are for sale to over a BILLION Internet users and over 40,000 social media sites. I enlist your site to major search engines and link to over a dozen other highly viewed sites. I feature you and your books and send out professionally created press releases, author platforms, and selling sheets to the targeted audience I have carefully researched. I establish followers in groups, exposing you and your books even more, until soon … there are thousands clicking into your site. Now, talk about massive exposure and the increased possibility of success in selling your books.

You've put all these days, perhaps years, into fulfilling your dream of publishing your book(s). Don't you deserve to have the opportunity to expose your pride and joy to the most people possible? At Premium Promotional Services *You Write – We Promote*.

Please check us out. If you have any questions, we will be more than happy to answer them.

WHERE YOU CAN FIND ME

ON THE INTERNET, I'm all over the place. I have profiles sitting in nearly 30 different social media sites, which I visit weekly. If you see me somewhere, please send out a friend request. I love the company, and I'm happy to share the knowledge I've gained along the way.

PREMIUM PROMOTIONAL SERVICES is the marketing and promotional business I started after realizing that many authors were dealt similar hands of fate ... too much to do and too little time to do it. The motto, *You Write – We Promote*, was quickly established. We discovered that many writers feel inadequate with the business and technical aspects of promoting themselves, and what starts out as a vision soon grows to be a hard reality. Thanks to my partner, Brian Knight, we run a productive promotional business that can serve the needs of our fellow writers. The list of endorsements on the site says it all. If you're searching for someone to do your promotional work, please visit the Premium Promotional Services site at:

http://www.premiumpromotions.biz

We can take care of ALL your marketing needs.

ON TUESDAYS at 11:00 AM (MST), I host a live show on BlogTalkRadio called "Authors Articulating." My guests and I have been accused of "sizzling with energy" as we discuss two main aspects of writing—alternating from "The Journey to Publication" to "Marketing Tips." During the second half of the show, you are welcome to call in as our guest, introduce yourself, and pitch your book. To listen to the live show, go to:

http://www.blogtalkradio.com/prempromotions

or become an active participant in our chat room at:

http://bit.ly/uuHfl

If you miss the show, no worries. A recording will be left as a BTR badge in my sidebar at one of my sites.

JOURNEY TO PUBLICATION is my personal site. I share my experiences as my dream to publish turns to reality. My novel, **Conquer All Obstacles,** is a suspense/romance—a special dedication to ALL who have struggled with a mental illness, the family and friends who have been affected by this disease, and to those women who are overcoming the trauma of violence. To follow this miraculous adventure, I invite you to ride along with me at:

http://www.joconquerall.com

All of the strategies included in *Premium Promotional Tips For Writers* came from published articles in my other personal blog called "**Marketing Tips for Authors**," with the theme, or brand, of: *Conquer All Obstacles*.

Additional entries are produced bi-weekly, so feel free to add more ideas to this book by visiting:

http://www.joconquerobstacles.com

I love to share the knowledge I have gained with fellow writers as I venture forth through more open doors.

In just over six months, as of September 1, 2009, my Facebook page bounced over 4,000 friends. Please join us by requesting my friendship. There is plenty to read and say within the comforts of a loving community of marvelous people. You can find me at:

http://www.facebook.com/joanne.vandermeulen

A phishing attack to Twitter, forced my account to disable. I started all over and now have a new Twitter account. I invite you to follow me at:

http://www.twitter.com/ppromotionals.net

To my family, friends, followers, and fans—a community filled with love—your constant presence is your gift to me. Thank you for your support. I am truly blessed.

———————

I praise the Lord, my Shepherd, for I am never alone.
Without Him, I am nothing.

You can *Conquer All Obstacles*,

—*Jo-Anne*

GLOSSARY

Google Alert: A service offered by Google, the search engine company, which notifies its users by e-mail, or as a feed, about the latest web and news pages of their choice.

Author Platform: Where you tell the world about yourself and your book.

Bit.ly: A utility that allows users to shorten the length of a URL and then track the resulting usage.

Blog: A term shortened from *weblog*, a type of website for journaling in chronological order with newest post first, usually by one person.

Blogger: Someone who makes posts to a blog, or blogger.com.

Blogging: Making a post to a blog.

Blog Platform: The software used to build and maintain your blog.

Blogroll: A list of blogs on a blog, usually placed in the sidebar, that is a list of recommendations by the blogger of other blogs.

Copyright: A law that gives you ownership over the things you create.

Dashboard: An interactive user interface that organizes and presents information in a way that is easy to read and manipulate.

E-Book: An electronic book, a digital file that readers can download from the Internet and read on a computer or a handheld device.

Editor: The person who puts a literary work into acceptable form.

HTML: HyperText Markup Language, the predominant computer language for building web pages.

HTML Code: The code used to build web pages.

Kindle: Amazon's wireless e-book reader.

KISS: An acronym for "Keep It Simple, Sweetie," or Silly, or Stupid.

Long Tailed Keywords: A combination of words making up a keyword phrase that helps narrow the selection category in a search engine.

Lurker: A person who reads blog discussions but never comments.

MetaTags: Keywords and descriptions embedded in HTML code to inform web crawlers about your page.

Niche: A certain interest group toward whom you will focus your efforts.

Ping: A utility used to test the delay between or to generate a response from one computer to another on a network or the Internet.

PodCast: A digital recording made available on the Internet for downloading to a personal audio player.

Post: An entry made to a blog.

Print On Demand (POD): A way of printing books from digital files for a fixed cost per copy, regardless of the size of the order.

Profile: The personal information about yourself that you provide during registration.

Publisher: The person or company responsible for the process of producing books. Includes overseeing the editing, design, production, printing, and sometimes the marketing of the book.

RSS Badge: A pagelet that allows visitors to easily find and subscribe to your site's RSS feed.

RSS Feed: Rich Site Summary, commonly called Really Simple Syndication, is a format for delivering regularly changing web content.

Self Publisher: The publishing of books by their authors.

Sidebar: The smaller columns to the left and/or right of the main center column on a blog page. Typically, widgets and a variety of links and information of the blogger's choice are added to the sidebars.

Signature: A body of text you choose to add to the end of a post.

Social Bookmark: A method for Internet users to share, organize, search, and manage bookmarks of web resources.

Tags: A keyword or term associated with or assigned to a piece of information.

Traffic: The number of visitors to a blog or website.

Tweet: A post or status update on Twitter.

URL: Uniform Resource Locator, the "address" of a web page.

Webcrawler: A computer program that browses the World Wide Web creating a copy of all the visited pages for later processing by search engines.

Widget: Small programs you can add to your website or blog; includes icons, pull-down menus, buttons, selection boxes, progress indicators, on-off checkmarks, scroll bars, windows, window edges (that let you resize the window), toggle buttons, forms, and many other devices for displaying information and for inviting, accepting, and responding to user actions.

PREMIUM PROMOTIONAL SERVICES
Your Promoting and Marketing Solution

You Write — We Promote

Site Creation • Advertising • Fan Pages • Book Promotion

Interviews • Site Redesign • Book Video

PREMIUM PROMOTIONAL SERVICES will give you an optimum online presence, guaranteed, exposing you and your book to millions of people who buy books online every day. Jo-Anne, Brian and Misty are eager and prepared to work with authors on a one-to-one basis for powerful, effective online promotion, marketing your book to give it the best chance at success.

PREMIUM PROMOTIONAL SERVICES will market you and your book(s) using effective and powerful promotional tactics. With the Internet promotional expertise to optimize search engines and generate streams of readers, your name and book(s) will surface to the top. Jo-Anne, Brian, and Misty will provide the vehicle, with you behind the wheel.

Hold on and enjoy the ride. Very soon you will be venturing into a journey of increased sales and profits.

WHO WE ARE:

Internet Promotional Manager Jo-Anne Vandermeulen understands that your book has to stand out from the pack and that technology can be daunting.

Website/Blog Specialist Brian Knight's expertise in redesigning your Author Domain will attract viewers. He understands the jargon in technology can be confusing.

Videographer Misty Taggart is available to create a professional video trailer, the most significant multi-media marketing tool you will ever invested in!

Each special service will give you enormous exposure. Millions of readers will notice your name and book(s).

info@ppromotionals.net
www.PremiumPromotions.biz

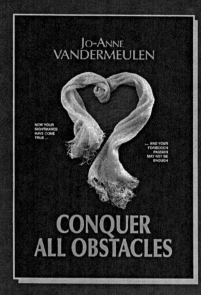

Title: **Conquer All Obstacles**
Author: **Jo-Anne Vandermeulen**
ISBN: **978-0-9841680-1-9**
Genre: **Suspense – Romance**
Pages: **256**
Available in **Paperback, Hard Cover, and eBook**
Reviewed By: **Brian Knight**
Official Premium Promotional Services Rating: **5-Star**

A WOMAN WHO WANTS TO FIND LOVE …

Middle-aged divorcee, Tara Robstead, wants more than a secret love affair with her boss, Josh Henderson.

WILL DO WHATEVER IT TAKES FOR A HAPPILY-EVER-AFTER …

Yet, her search for a happily-ever-after costs her more than a price paid in blood—her soul is slaughtered.

EVEN TANGLING WITH A PSYCHOPATH …

Now confined in a mental hospital, she must confront her greatest fears in order to break a psychopath's control over her fractured mind.

YET, LOVE HAS THE POWER TO …

Against the ticking clock, Josh must face his true love for Tara before it's too late.
Together, Tara and Josh can stand united to …

CONQUER ALL OBSTACLES

Order now from: **Vandermeulen.LaurusBooks.com**

JO-ANNE VANDERMEULEN

Owner and Marketeer of
PREMIUM PROMOTIONAL SERVICES
You Write – We Promote
www.premiumpromotions.biz

Professional Online Network Support
MARKETING TIPS FOR WRITERS
www.joconquerobstacles.com

Produces and Hosts a Live Radio Show
AUTHORS ARTICULATING
www.blogtalkradio.com/prempromotions

Prolific Author
• ***CONQUER ALL OBSTACLES*** (Suspense/Romance)
• ***PREMIUM PROMOTIONAL TIPS FOR WRITERS***
(Non-fiction/Resource)

Visit Her Personal Sites
Journey to Publication – www.joconquerall.com
Conquer All Obstacles – www.joconquerobstacles.com

Jo-Anne welcomes new fans to request friendship at:
www.facebook.com/joanne.vandermeulen

Alan Stupak, Photographer

JO-ANNE VANDERMEULEN

JO-ANNE VANDERMEULEN graduated from the University of Saskatchewan with a degree in Education and an English Literature major. She taught for the Moosomin School Division for twenty years before starting her full time writing career in 2006.

Jo-Anne produces and hosts a live weekly Blog Talk Radio (BTR) show, "Authors Articulating," where she shares marketing and promotional tips with other writers and answers questions from her extensive and ever-growing list of followers. She is owner of Premium Promotional Services, a company that supports and markets fellow writers.

Jo-Anne has two grown daughters and resides in Yorkton, Saskatchewan, with her husband, Randy, and their mini-dachshund, Oscar.